The Forest Town Hostel
1944 – 1959

by

Pauline & Malcolm Marples

'Memories for the Millennium'

by the

Nottinghamshire Living History Archive
Millennium Award Scheme

A MILLENNIUM AWARD SCHEME
SUPPORTED BY FUNDS
FROM THE NATIONAL LOTTERY

Nottinghamshire
County Council

City of
NOTTINGHAM

First Edition 2002

Published by the
"Nottinghamshire Living History Archive Millennium Award Scheme"

ISBN 1-904102-20-4

Copies of this book are made available through the Nottinghamshire County Libraries and the Nottingham City Libraries. This publication contains extracts from oral history interviews; full transcripts and audio recordings of these interviews are also available at selected libraries. Copies of the book may be available to purchase from the authors. Please contact the Local Studies Department of the Central Library, Angel Row, Nottingham NG1 6HP for further details.

Whilst every care has been taken to ensure the accuracy of the information contained in this publication, Nottinghamshire Living History Archive Millennium Award Scheme cannot accept responsibility for any error or omission. Attempts have been made to contact copyright holders where appropriate. If any have been inadvertently missed out, this will be rectified in future editions.

Printed by

Blue Print, Unit 3, Oakwood Road
Oak Tree Business Park, Mansfield, Notts. NG18 3HQ

CONTENTS

Abbreviations

NAO	Nottinghamshire Archive Office
NCB	National Coal Board
NUM	National Union of Mineworkers
PRO	Public Record Office

Notes

The book is based on oral history interviews and extracts from these have been used throughout. Spoken extracts are in inverted commas; these have been written as they have been said to indicate a person's dialect and personality.

Words in Italics denote the interviewer speaking.

Acknowledgements

This project would not have been possible without the help and encouragement of many people:

Dennis Hill, Samantha Holgate-Davey, Kevin Robson, and other members of the Nottinghamshire Living History Archive Millennium Award Team.

Interviewees:

Eileen M Armstrong, Albert Allott, Audrey Allott, Sheila Baker, Gracjan Borrys, William J Brown, Pawel Czarnecki, Charles Lewis Dery, E. Dunajewski, Brenda Flinders, Anna Gill, Frank Hanford, Molly Hanford, Josef Jurkiw, Les Keeling, Lily Kent, Eugen Megdalewitsch, Siegfied Nawrath, Jainos (John) Nugi, Julian Olexiuk, Monica Palmer, Mike Parkin, Ray Pollard, Iris A Ram, Pat Salmon, Brenda Sandor, Marjorie Smith, Joan Tate, Jack Wakefield, Jozef Wietrzychowski, Lionel George Wortley
Not forgetting spouses who offered hospitality, cups of tea and were wonderful at keeping quite while the tape recorder was on.

'The Forest Town Detectives' - Children in Class 11 (aged 7 & 8) at Forest Town Primary School. Also, Tim Bristow (Former Headteacher), Garry Ineson (Head Teacher), Joy Bramall (Teacher) plus other Staff and helpers.

Shirley Blythe, Chris Kidger, Freda Walmsley, Rene Martin, Thelma Pothecary, Rhoda Cope, Olive Oldfield, Hilda Moxon, Elizabeth Richardson, Audrey Todd, Mr Lambeth, Jim Turner, John Danbury, John Newton, Phylis Newton. Arthur Parker, Mr Vanags (Snr), John Vanags, Mr Wardle, Trudy Smith, Harry Bowler, Jeanne Smith, Joan Wilson, Gwen Beaumont, Sylvia Roberts, Mick Flook, Derek Flowers, Janice Jackson, Elaine Jelley, Ann Kimberly, Eric Gripton, Jill Taylor, Margaret Ward, David Ward, J Alderson, Charlie Travers, Ted Swaby, and many others.

Members of Kingsway Community Project, Monday Club, Forest Town
Attendees at the Forest Town Slide Shows, also other venues we have visited and publicised this project.

Warwick H Taylor, Bevin Boys Association

Bob Haughton, Chief Executive National Centre for Young People with Epilepsy

Keith Newman Editor NARPO
Ray Hadley NARPO
Inspector Dave Shardlow, and other Police Officers, Forest Town Police Station
David Storer, Media & Public Relations, Nottinghamshire Police Head Quarters, Sherwood Lodge Nottingham
Helen Elliott, Barbara Hicks, Bob Foster Media & Public Relations West Yorkshire Police, Wakefield

Curators & Staff Mansfield Museum & Art Gallery

Staff at Eden Camp Museum, Malton Yorkshire

Staff at Forest Town Library; Mansfield Local Studies Library; Nottingham Local Studies Library, Sutton in Ashfield Library.

Staff at Nottingham Archive Office, Rotherham Archive Office, Surrey History Centre, Public Record Office.

Mansfield District Council - various Departments
Nottingham County Council Technical Library and other Departments

Jeremy Plews, Editor 'Chad' North Notts Newspapers Ltd

People who have contributed photographs and documents.

There are so many individual people who have passed on information, or the names of people to contact it is impossible to name them all.

To everyone we do say 'Thank You' your contribution has been invaluable.

Pauline & Malcolm

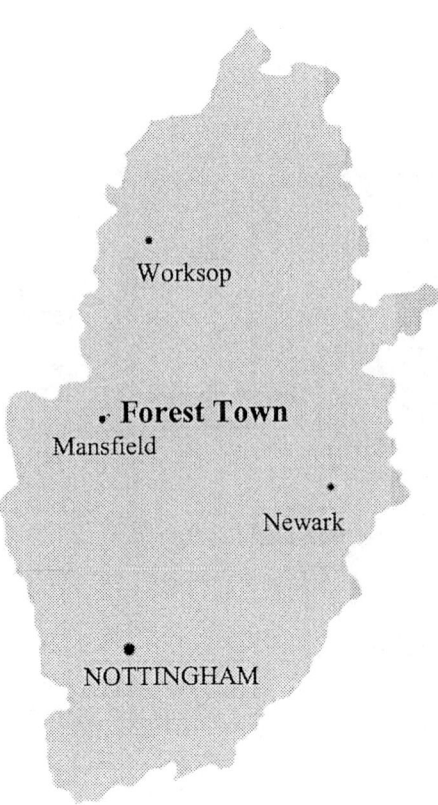

Location of Forest Town within Nottinghamshire

Forest Town Primary School Children
Investigating the area today [November 2001] for signs of the past

INTRODUCTION

This is the story of the Forest Town Hostel, a place that dominated our local landscape in the middle of the twentieth century, and which is still remembered by people who lived in the area at that time. The greatest majority of local residents however, have no knowledge of the Hostel complex and yet it played a significant part in both our local and national history. For this reason, it is important that neither the buildings, nor the people who resided there, are forgotten.

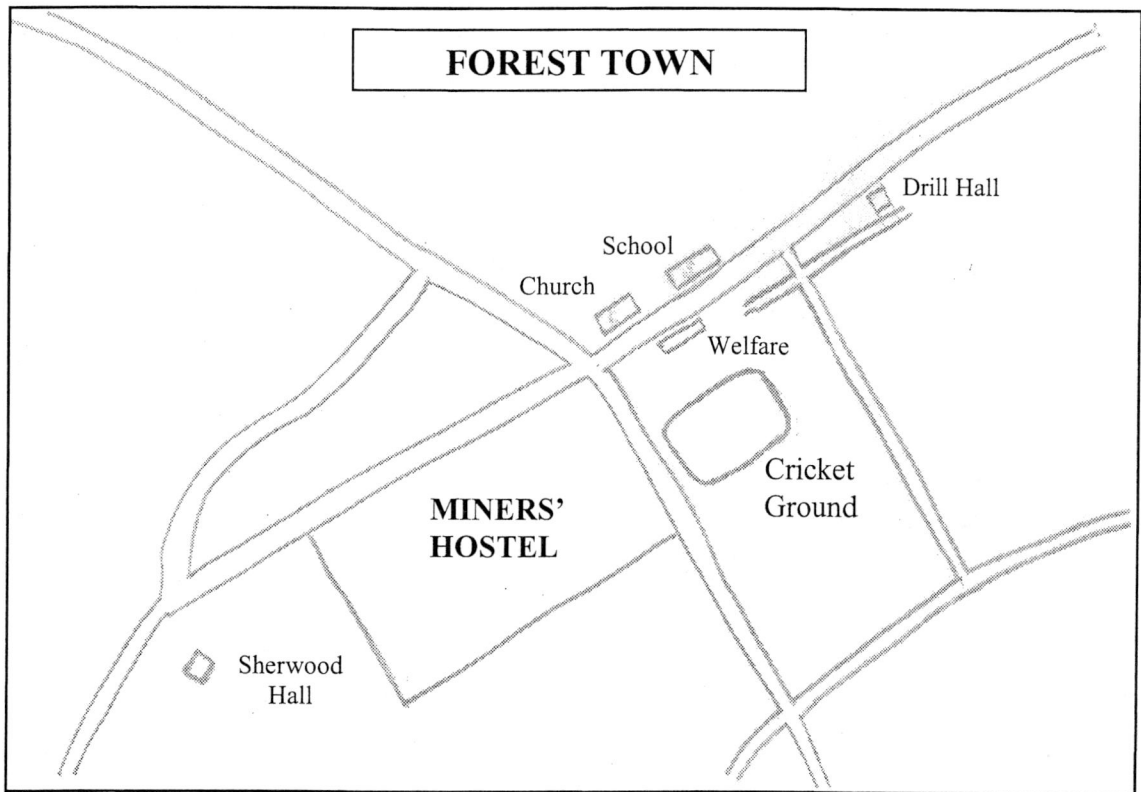

Today, on the land where the Hostel once stood there are many buildings: houses, bungalows, a library, health centre and police station. There is no indication though of what was there before they were built. The children of Forest Town Primary School visited the site in November 2001 to investigate and look for clues. Despite enthusiastically walking round the buildings, examining the structures and peeling paint all they found was a plaque on the Police Station that revealed the date 1965.

The date was a starting point and like the children we were keen to find out more, to take a journey back in time, to ask questions, search documents, and record people's memories. Initial inquiries among local people suggested there had once been a camp or a hostel. There were however many variations of the people who had lived there. It was left with us to discover who the occupants really were, and what had brought them to Forest Town.

The Millennium Living History Archive Award provided the opportunity and means for us to do this, albeit in a very limited time scale. This has narrowed the scope of what could be done but it has still been a rewarding and exciting project. Visits and contacts have been made to various libraries and archives including the PRO at Kew and additional contact with librarians, archivists and other knowledgeable people has been made. Thirty-one people have been tape-recorded, their memories were invaluable to the project.

While we are aware that there is still more information to discover, and many additional people who have an interesting story to tell, this book is the first step in recording a very intriguing part of both our local and national history.

* * * * * * * * * * * * * * * * * *

The years from 1939 –1945 was the period of the Second World War. It was a distressing time when fighting, destruction and unspeakable atrocities occurred. Families were torn apart. Fear prevailed and the death toll rose daily. Bombs devastated parts of Britain, and children were evacuated to 'safe' areas. People were encouraged to 'dig for victory' and grow vegetables, as food became scarce. Food rationing began in 1940. The following year clothing rationing was introduced. Queuing and 'make do and mend' became a way of life. More rationing was to follow and people had to adjust accordingly.

Industry suffered from a shortage of essential supplies and manpower. As more men volunteered or were conscripted into military service, women replaced them in factories, on the land, and elsewhere. Wherever possible people were rallied to the cause, the needs of the country were important. One essential product during those war years was coal. It was needed to keep the wheels of industry turning and to enable the continuation of necessary supplies such as steel to be produced.

Coal mines at this time were in private ownership and the coal industry was very short of manpower. Many men were already serving their country in the various military forces. Others left the coal pits, attracted by the offer of better working conditions and higher pay, they began work in other industries employed on war work. In May 1940 about 760,000 men were on the colliery books, this was not enough, the coal output had to be raised. It was estimated an additional 40,000 workers were needed.[1] The government had to consider ways to rectify this and various schemes were put into operation.

 Appeals were made over the radio for ex-miners to return to work in the coal mines. Opportunities were created for former miners to leave the forces and return to the pits. For some colliery workers coal mining was made a reserved occupation. The initial schemes did not have the desired effect the government had hoped for and a Mining Optants Scheme was brought into operation. As an alternative to serving in H.M. Forces, men under the age of twenty five who were required to register, were given the alternative of working in the coal mines underground. The age limit was discarded when still not enough men came forward, it was an option that remained in force until the end of the European War.

Despite all the new ideas put into operation, appeals on the radio, letters to headmasters requesting they make school leavers aware 'they were needed in the coal industry to help with the war', there was still a manpower shortage. A decision was taken, and in December 1943 the Right Hon. Ernest Bevin, Minister of Labour and National Service, announced a new scheme. It was the start of the 'Bevin Boy' era and it changed the lives of thousands of young men.

Young men, who between the age of eighteen and twenty five were required to register for the Armed Forces, were now subject to a ballot, this could mean their 'war' was spent working in the coal mines, not in military action. The majority did not have an option.[2] For many young men who had anticipated wearing a uniform and fighting for their country, wearing a pit helmet and digging coal for the war effort was no consolation.[3] For them it was a devastating decision, their lives were changed in a way they had never anticipated. These young men became known as Bevin Boys[4] and were sent to various coal mining areas to live, train and work. For some this was Nottinghamshire and a place called Forest Town.

Notes

[1]   Taylor W *The Forgotten Conscript* (Durham 1988) p 1
[2]   Taylor W *The Forgotten Conscript* (Durham 1988) p 4
[3]   For further reading on this subject the above book, is recommended.
[4]   Named after the Right Hon. Ernest Bevin, Minister of Labour and National Service

THE HOSTEL

Once the decision was made to conscript new mining trainees, accommodation for them to live had to be found. Initially some men were billeted in peoples homes after requests were made in local newspapers, however more permanent plans had to be made and Mining Hostels were established. In Forest Town, several local people recalled that plans had already been agreed to build homes on the green field site in the vicinity of the crossroads. The land however was requisitioned to build the Miners' Hostel, and instead of houses or bungalows, new plans were made to erect rows of Nissen Huts,[1] large semicircular corrugated steel buildings that would each accommodate twelve men. As work on the new construction started local people were unsure what it was to be. Two young lads at that time recall:

> "I can remember when they was building it. There was rumours in the village that it could be an Army camp, it could be a prisoner of war camp, it could be all sorts of things, until we finally learnt that it was going to be for the Bevin Boys. That was in about 1943/44 that sort of period, and I can remember it being built."[2]

> "I lived on what was then called Sherwood Hall, better known now as Clipstone Road West, and lived right opposite what became known as the Bevin Boys Camp…I can remember a cornfield being there and looking at that from our sitting room window. Later on I remember the camp being there."[3]

A Snow Covered Hostel (camp) on Clipstone Road.
Looking towards Forest Town crossroads – February 1958

In February 1944 the Ministry of Works and Supplies Division produced a 'Schedule of Furniture and Equipment for 500 Person Type Hostel.'[4] This gave the typical layout of the huts with locker units for a Nissen Hut with twelve beds. Illustrations of furniture are shown for the canteen, recreation room and reveal that higher grades of staff had better furniture. Equipment lists give an added insight into the accommodation at the Miners' Hostel: - These included Living Hut Blocks with an Entrance and Corridors, Locker Room, Bath Houses, Lavatories, Box and Linen Room, Storekeepers Block. Additionally there was a Welfare Centre, and Recreation Room. There were rooms for the staff, and a Manager's Bungalow.

The following has been extracted from the Schedule:

Entrance and Corridors

		£	s	d
8	Notice Boards 3' x 2'	5	3	4
8	Refuse Bins 24" x 18"	3	12	8

Locker Room

		£	s	d
8	Sets Boot Cleaning Brushes (Sets of 3)	1	3	8
4	Mirrors 13½" x 10½"		15	0
56	Forms 4' 8"	42	0	0
2	Tables, Folding 4' 6" (for Attendants)	3	6	0

Lavatories

		£	s	d
48	Holders, Toilet Roll	2	12	0
48	Hooks		17	0
48	Mirrors	9	0	0

Bath Houses

		£	s	d
24	Chairs, Fold Flat	12	2	0
24	Door Hooks		8	6
24	Bath Mats	3	10	0

Kitchen Equipment

			£	s	d
6	Brushes,	Nail		5	3
24	"	Scrubbing	1	8	6
4	"	Pastry		6	7
6	"	Saucepan		4	9
6	"	Sink		3	6
3	"	Stove, hard		3	11
3	"	Stove, soft		10	1
12	"	for Urn Taps		12	0
96	Cloths,	Oven	6	2	0
144	"	Tea	14	8	0

Storekeepers Block

		£	s	d
504	Ash Trays	10	10	0
504	Mats, coco [coconut] matting 4' x 2' 3" fancy	107	2	0
2,1116	Blankets (4 per person plus 5% spares)	1,639	18	0
1,028	Pillows (2 per person plus 2% spares)	124	4	4
1,588	Sheets single (3 per person 5% spares)	542	11	4
1,588	Slips, Pillow (3 per person 5% spares)	92	12	8
1,588	Towels, Terry (plus 55 spares)	100	18	1

Standard 2' 6" folding beds with pallets [mattresses] were the standard equipment. Coat hangers with and without trouser rails were provided. While toothbrushes, beakers, soap and soap dishes are listed as toilet issue, there does not appear to be any mention of shaving tackle. For the miners' locker units, padlocks were also provided.

Despite the country still being at war and the population being told of shortages and rationing, the list of kitchen utensils suggest they were well equipped.[5] Eileen, a pastry cook who worked at the Forest Town Miners' Hostel when it first opened remembered:

> "Kitchen? Well it was very nice, the ovens…one on top and one underneath. Everything you wanted you got, your electric mixers and everything, …big rollers and pastries everything, it was very nice…And then you got…the big kitchen with all the big, well pans, they were vessels that you did the vegetables in. I mean they were this high, [demonstrates three or four feet high]…I think there were four or five of those…"

There was more than one kitchen, each with their own ovens, and plenty of meals to be prepared.

> "I had a separate pastry kitchen. Then when I wasn't busy doing that I used to go and help out in the big kitchen…you see you've got to have meals for those going on afternoon shift, you've got to give them a cooked meal. You'd got some of 'em coming home early in the morning, so you'd got to be there to give them a hot meal between one and three in a morning. Then you'd got some coming off the afternoon shift, ten or eleven, you'd got to have another cooked meal ready for them then…So it was all sort of all-go all the time…Well, we didn't work twenty four hours 'cause there was shifts you see."[6]

In the miners' hostels managed by the National Service Hostels Corporation Limited there were of course many people to cater for and the hostel was built to accommodate both staff and miners. While outside the appearance was that of an Army barracks inside it was:

> "…nice an' beautiful and clean, it was a really nice hostel, it was."

> *Can you remember any of the colours, or how was it decorated, was it fairly plain?*

> "Yes your bedrooms was lovely and clean, everything was…they was the Nissen Huts type, with nice curtains and everything up and you felt at home really."[7]

The Forest Town Hostel was built to accommodate 500 men and additional staff.[8] The first of these were conscripted miners, better known as Bevin Boys. However they were just one fraction of the Hostel's occupants over the next fifteen years.

Notes

[1]   Named after Col Peter Nissen (1871 –1930) Inventor & British Mining Engineer
[2]   Les Keeling
[3]   Mike Parkin
[4]   PRO Works 22/186
[5]   See Appendix
[6]   Eileen M Armstrong
[7]   Eileen M Armstrong
[8]   There are variations on this figure - early newspaper reports say 500. Different documents in PRO Coal 23/369 give 600 & 816

One of the displays at Eden Camp, Malton, North Yorkshire

THE BEVIN BOY ERA

The decision to conscript Bevin Boys to the pits was made in December 1943. By January 1944 headlines began to appear in the Mansfield newspapers:

'Miner Trainees - Six Hundred Billets Required In Mansfield'

They told how young men being drafted into the mining industry under the 'call up scheme' would first attend the Cresswell Training Centre [Derbyshire], and then be directed to local collieries. Mr S Wadsworth, the Chief Billeting Officer, stressed that finding accommodation for the trainees was a matter of national urgency. Mr I E Pickard, the Mayor of Mansfield additionally requested the support of local people to take the young men into their homes. The suggested amount of 30/- to 35/- [£1.50 to £1.75] weekly board to be paid, may have encouraged some people to take in a lodger.[1]

Newly conscripted Bevin Boys who were designated to work in South Derbyshire and North Nottinghamshire, were sent by train to Chesterfield. From there they were taken by bus to surrounding communities where they were to lodge. By the second week in February the first batch of forty trainees had arrived at Mansfield Woodhouse. Among the welcoming committee at the Turner Hall were, Mr H B Taylor (MP), J T Rice (Manager of the Mansfield Colliery), Councillors Wilcox and Poole, and Rev D H Mortimer (Vicar of Forest Town).[2]

A week later at the British Restaurant in Belvedere Street, the Mayor and other civic dignitaries welcomed the first party of Bevin Boys to Mansfield. The men were told of the local amenities including the library, museum, technical college and Sherwood Forest. It was hoped that the men would make friends, and have 'many happy memories of the time they spent in Mansfield while playing their part in the war.'[3] The latter comment is ironic for Bevin Boys did not receive any kind of recognition for their war service, until 1995.[4]

The Bevin Boys were from all walks of life. They had worked as bank clerks, civil servants, grocers, butchers and in many other occupations. They came from all parts of the country, some were quick to make friends and make the best of the new life to which they had been allotted.

Bert Allott was one of these young men, he lived in Grimsby where he worked as a lorry driver, delivering food for a wholesale grocer. It was a job he enjoyed, but like many other young men Bert was 'called up' and in January 1944, the pattern of his life changed.

"I wanted to go in the Navy 'cos me dad were a fisherman."

So, you wanted to enlist in the Navy, you went to sign on, and what happened?

"Well I was medically examined, and I passed A1…then a letter came afterwards saying that I'd got to report to the mines, and that I'd got to be at Chesterfield on a certain day."

So how did you feel…because you had got to go in the mines and not in the Navy?

"Well I felt a bit gutted, but I decided that if I'd got to go I'd got to go and that's it, so when the letter came I went.

I were really wondering what the pits were gonna be like to tell you the truth, and I wasn't relishing it."[5]

Bert was conscripted to the mines in 1944, and on the day he caught the train to start his new life another young chap also got on at Great Coates, just outside Grimsby. He was Les Attcliffe. Bert and Les soon discovered they were both going to Chesterfield, to work in the pits. "We got talking and we landed up in digs together at Forest Town after we'd been to Chesterfield."

At Chesterfield Bert recalled they were met by the Mayor who "shook our hands and wished us all the best, and everything."

"We were going to Creswell, to work down the mine, Creswell Pit. And when we got there we were taken to digs, and Les Attcliffe and myself, we got digs together, we were there six months training to be a miner. The worst trouble was walking about with these big pit boots on, and we used to sing a song, summat about 'great big boots and blisters on ya feet, sent to join Bevin's army'.

We used to be walking around Creswell Crags, and march along to get used to the boots, 'cos we'd never wore boots, we always wore shoes. Anyway, we had our digs in the village at Clowne, we lived at Clowne, worked at Creswell, and bathed at Whitwell, when we got dirty. That's how it went on for six months, and then we were sent to our respective collieries. Crown Farm was the one that Les Attcliffe and I went to."[6]

Both men were sent to Forest Town where the policeman known as 'Bobby Weaver', told them "Oh I've got digs for yo' and I've got digs for yo." Bert learnt he was to stay with Bill Hilton in Seventh Avenue and Les with a family in Ninth Avenue. Though preliminary work had started on the Forest Town Hostel,[7] when the first Bevin Boys came to work at local collieries, it was not built.

It was 27th May 1944[8] when the Hostel built on land on the Sherwood Hall Estate eventually opened. Bert Allott and his work colleague Alec Taylor were two of the early occupants. Alec had hoped to lodge in the same digs as Bert on Seventh Avenue, but as the room was needed for Bill Hilton's daughters, the two young men both decided to move to the Hostel. They discovered the Hostel was a nice place:

"Well it were all brand new. Everything were alright, you know. You couldn't grumble. Food were good, and well I were satisfied, I don't know about some of the others."[9]

One lady, who tried to ensure the food was good, was Eileen Armstrong, she recalled:

"When the war first broke out, [aged fifteen or sixteen] I worked in a bake house…we did all the Naafis and looked after the forces that was at Hardwick and all round. We made all the cakes, and everything for them and we used to take them there. …Then it came that you'd got to do something for your country…so they [Dole Office] wanted me to go and look after children, but instead of that they decided…as they wanted cooks at the hostel, that it would be better to let me go there. Me mum was a widow, my brother was in the Navy and they thought I could stay at home and be near me mum…

…So I went as an assistant pastry cook, which, of course they didn't hire anybody else did they? Just myself, I was assistant to myself. That was when the camp first opened."

At the Hostel Eileen's job entailed working shifts, and even though her home was in the Avenues, just a short distance away, she had her own room and slept in.

"A nice little room with your own wardrobe, bed and a dressing table, carpeted, it was very nice…I made friends with one or two, I can remember Sally Wonacote, she came from Clipstone, she worked there. She was a cook, assistant, you know, serving things. The chef, he came from Nottingham…he was an elderly gentleman. …They all lived in. …Very often we used to meet at night and have a drink at the Ravensdale Hotel. …Of course we had everything to prepare for the miners after their shift. …they used to able to go and get a snack, 'cause they paid for that one, that wasn't free, the meals was, but the extras at evening time they paid for that, the cakes and the sandwiches, and coffee and tea, such as that."

The main meals were included as part of the miners board [accommodation rent], and to ensure there was always food for the hungry miners, the staff worked shifts. Some had to get up early:

"We used to have the chappie come and wake us up in the morning, right, half asleep! Yes we enjoyed it, we used to mix with the Bevin Boys, have a chat and a laugh and it was quite pleasant really. They were a nice lot of chappies, they were really. You'd get to know them all."

Were you encouraged to mix with them or was there no problem on that?

"No, no problem whatsoever. I mean you got to know them and you were very friendly with them. Sometimes they'd say 'We'll have the usual,' you know…tell you what they didn't like, and what they did like. You'd have a busy day making all sorts of things, teacakes, cakes, Yorkshire puddings."

Where did they actually work?

"The miners…well some worked at Crown Farm, some worked at Rufford, some of 'em went to Sherwood. I'm not sure whether any came to Ollerton, but there was Bilsthorpe and all round…Yes, quite a spread, there was quite a lot of Bevin Boys. They used to sit sometimes, the married men, and talk about their wives and their families, you felt as though you'd got to know them all. It was nice."[10]

Many of the Bevin Boys were young, unmarried and for some it would be the first time they had left home.

"They were all good lads you know. We were only young and nobody wanted to get into trouble or anything. So we'd just go to work and come back and, er just talk…I suppose like being in the forces. You had to make your own amusement and talk with whoever, or do what you want, whatever suited you. I expect some of us could have gone boozing if they'd [we'd] got the money."[11]

"The Bevin Boys you know just used to go out…just used to make their own amusement. There wasn't much to do then because you know there wasn't much money about and it were blackout, no there wasn't much. They just used to go to the Drill Hall for dances and things like that, I expect there were those who did have a drink."[12]

The Drill Hall [now Kingsway Hall]

The men were not allowed to invite women in the dormitories, and it is unclear if any dances or any other entertainment was provided at the hostel for them at that time.

"I don't think many came up from the village, but they'd meet if they went into the Ravensdale. It was a very popular place for them to go and meet and there was games for 'em to play, so they was quite happy…go in to Mansfield if they wanted to, they could do what they liked really. …they made their own entertainment inside, when there was evenings, …having their coffees and teas, and whatever they wanted…some of 'em did a bit of singing and, you know, that sort of thing…We didn't have a stage or anything like that…it was a very big room for them to sit in, you know, chairs and tables, they enjoyed it, it was quite comfortable. …"[13]

"You could do table tennis and snooker…boxing, if you wanted to do a bit of boxing. There were darts, there were all sorts if you wanted it."[14]

Inevitably some local girls married Bevin Boys who had come to stay in Forest Town. Among these were Audrey Taylor and Bert Allott, Frank Haynes[15] and Vera Lancaster, Irene Jelley and Jimmy Graves, Gwen [surname unknown] and Les Attcliffe. They continued to work and live in the area after the war.

For some people however, being a Bevin Boy was a different story, it meant separation from a wife and children. Iris Ram recalls how Raj, her husband came to Forest Town.

> "Raj was a fireman during the war, the whole of the war until 1944, when…because of the lack of bombs over the Midlands and the coast, he came, had to come as a Bevin Boy. …He was in the fire service from June 1939 until December 1944, when he had to come into the mines as a Bevin Boy, which was a big shock really to all of us."

> *Why did Raj go into the fire service?*

> "Well he wanted to go in the Navy, but they told him that he was too old for regular service, which was rather ironic because they were taking them in the thirties, later on during the war. That was the reason that he volunteered for the fire service in June 1939 before the war started. He was twenty-three."[16]

Iris and Raj lived in Skegness, they had first met when Raj who came from a village just outside Agra in the United Provinces India, was working as a trick cyclist at the Indian Theatre under the pier at Skegness.

It was Christmas 1944, when Raj was sent as a Bevin Boy to do six weeks training at Creswell, and then to work at Mansfield Colliery [often known as Crownie]. He stayed at the Abbott Road Miners' Hostel before eventually moving to the one at Forest Town, where he

Raja Ram – in his Fire Service uniform with the family pet

lived for a number of years, and possibly because of the length of time he stayed there Raj always referred to it as the Polish Camp. Like a number of the Bevin Boys, when the opportunity came to give up their jobs in the coal mines, he didn't.

> "He decided that he was going to stay. I was rather surprised, because he'd never been used to manual work, not heavy work like that and I was rather surprised, but he decided he was going to stay. We found it very difficult to get a house…we tried to get a house up here, but I think personally it was because of Raj's colour. I do feel that people were prejudiced, and it wasn't until 1953 that we were able to get a house. That was rather a long time with Raj coming home every week-end to Skegness on his motorbike. He came home every weekend even in the worst of the winter of 1947. I think he only missed one weekend…He would sometimes just have a couple of hours at home and he would be very cold and very wet. He'd say, well I wanted to come home to see you and the children."[17]

> *How did Raj keep in touch. Was it just the weekend visit?*

Raja Ram's Identity Card showing movement between the Miners Hostels

"No, we had a phone installed, so that he could let me know when he got home [back] safely. In 1947, no buses got through and he came home [to Skegness]...so it was very handy to have the phone just as a comfort really, to know that he'd arrived home [back to the Hostel]."[18]

Despite Bevin Boys having no option about the occupation that was forced upon them as being their war service, not everyone was sympathetic about this. Because the young men were not in uniform, some people chose to refer to them as conscientious objectors, or call up dodgers. Sadly even today this is still occasionally misquoted. However 'facts show that there were only 41 out of a total of 47,859 Bevin Boys'[19] who were sent to work in the coal mines because they were conscientious objectors.

Iris Ram did not recall her husband Raj having any problems because he was a Bevin Boy.

"I think that he got on very well really with them...I don't think he had any trouble with the miners at all. They were rather intrigued I think about the fact that he had his motorbike and was a bit of a mad cap on it...they've...told me stories about how fast he used to go up the Pit Lane...yes I think he got on quite well.

He bought the motorbike so that he could come home at weekends. He had a B.S.A, he had a Norton, and then he ended up with the then 'elite' of motorbikes, which was the Brough Superior 1000 cc, so of course he could really go, with that."[20]

Bert Allott still remembers those early years as a Bevin Boy at Crown Farm Colliery.

> "I worked on the pit top for a start, and Mr Hilton, Bill, were in the fire holes. ...there were a lot of snow to be shifted 'cos it were in the winter time, and I, I shifted snow and then oh I worked on the pit top, doggin-on or tekin couplings from between tubs as they went round when they were full. ...Then I worked down the pit in the pit bottom; and then I went er went further up the roads. ...I went on haulage, and I worked with Gilbert Higginbottom. ...So anyway, I got on the face and was cleaning up in front of the cutter, and it's just debris that just falls down off the side and top of the coal. It falls off, falls back, and we clean it up so that the cutter can come through to cut the face, so that colliers could come and clean it up and then the erectors and dismantlers could come to move the belts over for the next shift. After that I worked with Albert Tyers, a local chap."

While Bert recognised and got on with his allotted work in the pits as his 'war work' he was aware that while it was never said personally to him, there were comments made by one or two in relation to conscientious objectors. It was a situation he felt it was better not to get in to arguments about but inwardly

> "I felt narked. I felt mad. Why should I be called one of them. Because it were a bad thing to be said about people."

Because what you really wanted was to be in the forces?

> "YES"

No matter what occupation people were in, when the end of the war was declared there were many celebrations both nationally and locally. One person recalled that miners at the Hostel had a bonfire, and burnt their beds, however this has not been confirmed. The Mansfield Chronicle in June 1945 did report that a Victory Dance was held at the Hostel in Forest Town and the dining hall was 'decorated and be-flagged for the occasion.'[21] Mrs G Hilton the Hostel Welfare Officer and the residents committee organised the event. Among the 300 residents, staff, and guests at the event, were members of the Forces and the Women's Land Army.[22] Not surprisingly 'the hall was filled with happy couples.'[23] Stanley Day, a Bevin Boy (from Gravesend) was the MC, he was assisted by Bruce Walker.

The resident manager Mr G Vincent Day referred to the Bevin Boys in the Forest Town Hostel as a 'grand bunch of boys.'[24] However grand they were they must have been very disillusioned by the lack of recognition for their war service. Unlike people who had worn a uniform and served in the military forces, the Bevin Boys were never officially de-mobbed. They were sent letters encouraging them to remain in the industry, and as Bert recalls

> "We were told that we could go back, if we wished...it wasn't an official paper to sign. I can't remember signing a paper to say that I were de-mobbed, but I know as regards going back and finishing with the pit I could have done it when the war was over."[25]

By that time however this young Bevin Boy was married, and Forest Town was his home. It was many years before Bert and others like him were to be recognised for the important part they played in the Second World War.[26]

The Bevin Boy era at Forest Town was a mixed one, for within two months of moving into the hostel that had been built for them, the occupants had been moved to another hostel on Abbott Road, Mansfield. The Forest Town accommodation was needed for epileptic children who were being evacuated from Lingfield in Surrey. The following year in March 1945, after the children had returned to Surrey, the Hostel once more re-opened for the Bevin Boys.[27] However by the 17th August they were again moved back to the Abbott Road Hostel, as the buildings at Forest Town were needed by the Home Office to be used as a Police Training Centre. It was another two years before the large complex of Nissen Huts would again accommodate coal miners.

Memorial Plaque
in the Chapel, Eden Camp, Malton Yorkshire

Notes

[1]   Mansfield & North Notts Advertiser 28 January 1944
[2]   Mansfield & North Notts Advertiser 11 February 1944
[3]   Mansfield & North Notts Advertiser 18 February 1944
[4]   50th Anniversary of VE Day in London in speeches made by Her Majesty the Queen., the Rt. Hon Betty Boothroyd MP., Speaker of the House of Commons and the Rt. Hon John Major MP., Prime Minister
[5]   Albert (Bert) Allott
[6]   Albert (Bert) Allott
[7]   Mansfield & Kirkby Chronicle 27 Jan 1944
[8]   PRO LAB 22/63
[9]   Albert (Bert) Allott
[10]   Eileen M Armstrong
[11]   Albert (Bert) Allott
[12]   Audrey Allott
[13]   Eileen M Armstrong
[14]   Albert (Bert) Allott
[15]   Frank Haynes MP., JP., Ashfield
[16]   Iris Ram
[17]   Iris Ram
[18]   Iris Ram
[19]   Taylor W. *The Forgotten Conscript*
[20]   Iris Ram
[21]   Mansfield Chronicle 14 June 1945
[22]   There was a Women's Land Army Hostel at Old Clipstone
[23]   Mansfield Chronicle 14 June 1945
[24]   Mansfield Chronicle 14 June 1945
[25]   Albert (Bert) Allott
[26]   As Note 4
[27]   PRO LAB 22/63

EPILEPTIC EVACUEES

During the Second World War, Forest Town like the rest of the country was encouraged to take precautions against enemy invasion. Blackout curtains had to be at windows, car headlamps masked, gas masks carried, and the village school was prepared for emergencies. The school logbook discloses, 'gas mask delivery[1]...rehearsal fitting gas masks[2]...this morning gas mask drill was taken in all the classrooms and the scatter scheme was practised.'[3] While the village was subject to many air raid warnings especially at the end of 1940 and early in 1941,[4] Forest Town did not suffer from enemy bombing, unlike many other areas of the country from where children had to be evacuated.

Forest Town was a reception area for evacuees. In September 1940 a large number of children arrived from Southend.[5] The following March, 135 children aged from five to eleven arrived from Worthing.[6] Children were admitted to the village School.[7] Those evacuated children were found homes with families and they were able to mix and play with local children.

'Doodlebug' at Eden Camp

In 1944 pilotless flying bombs, known as 'Doodlebugs' started to devastate areas around London and the South. Children were once again being evacuated. A special residential school in Surrey known as the Lingfield Epileptic Colony had so far survived the war with the minimum of disruption. That was until an appearance of the flying bomb. In June 1944 a bomb fell on the colony, causing vast destruction to three of the girl's homes and to the hospital block. Sixty of the girls were injured in this attack. Ten weeks later when two of the boys homes were hit by another bomb, the running of the school was considered to be virtually impossible, and a decision was made to evacuate the children and staff. They were offered the use of accommodation in Nottinghamshire, at the Bevin Boys Hostel in Forest Town.

With less than two days notice 150 boys, (plus necessary equipment) travelled by coach, ambulance, and lorry to Forest Town. They were followed two days later by 85 girls. Additionally 45 staff accompanied the children.[8] After leaving the open countryside and relative spaciousness of their Surrey accommodation, arrival at their new Forest Town home would have been rather strange.

View of Nissen Huts with Pit Headstocks in the background.

The rows of large black Nissen Huts, with distant views of headstocks, and the tall chimney of Mansfield Colliery must have been an awesome sight to both the children and the staff.

At this time there were still evacuees from Worthing integrated in the local community and attending the village school. The sudden arrival of a whole school of children with specialist needs descending on the village, to live in the barrack-type complex must have been rather strange. Their transport and mode of travel would additionally have been rather an unusual sight in the village, and no one seems to have recollections of these.

The sparse Nissen Hut accommodation was not ideal for the epileptic children. Large areas of concrete surfaces both inside and outside the huts added to the dangers for children if they fell. However, despite a lack of grassed area for the children's educational needs, and a change to the residential school routine, both the children and staff adjusted to the new life. There is no evidence of communication with the local school, and yet the Lingfield children were said to have benefitted from an increase in both quantity, and quality of books. Just where these were supplied from is unknown.[9]

In the 1940s there was less understanding of epilepsy than there is today, and in Forest Town, while there was both sympathy and understanding for the children, there was also a little fear, especially from people who at that time, were only very young themselves:

> "...They used to come to church. There were three or four rows of 'em with helmets on, and I was terrified out of my life with them...Well we wondered what they were, I mean it was such a terrible name this epileptic colony."[10]

Another person recalled her feelings when she first went to help with the children at the hostel,

> "Well a little bit when I started to go of fear, you know having not come across anything like that before, but I was made very welcome."[11]

Seeing some of the children wearing protective headgear was obviously unusual and this has stayed in people's memories for nearly 60 years;[12]

> "...Some of them wore like sponge things round their head...in case they fell and they injured themselves,"[13]

> "I don't remember any particular uniform, but I do remember them wearing a particular type of headgear to protect themselves, ...it looked similar to the headgear that a racing cyclist would have worn in that period of time."[14]

> "Some were confined to wheelchairs, others wore huge protective rubber hoops round their heads to save them from serious injury during a fit."[15]

However people soon got used to seeing the children walking around the village, or just at play like Brenda did when she visited her friend Mary.

'Goochies Wood' on Pump Hollow Lane
[Date unknown]

"Well you would see them but I don't ever remember 'em walking around the village but you see I lived this side, [of the village] and they was that side. You only met... if you played in Goochies Woods, which we often did."[16]

Goochies Wood, otherwise known as Crookies Wood to some people, was just below the hostel site.

"They were brought out as a group and they usually walked hand in hand, sort of snake fashion, not that there was a lot of traffic around at that time anyway, but I presumed just to make sure they were secure and under the eye of the teachers. ...As far as I know, I think they just stayed within the camp and we just saw them if you like, exercising outside when they were walked every day, and then back to the camp."[17]

"Well I can remember the children who were epileptics, and they came into the village, ...I can remember they brought them in groups, to what we call... Queensway Park, but it was always referred to as the playfield...swings and roundabouts and everything on there...but we never had a lot to do with them personally. We never got to know them really."[18]

Some people however did get to know the children, and any fears that they had were soon overcome. Young people from church youth groups, and the girl guides befriended the children and many happy memories have remained with them.

'Well I should say they were from about twelve to about fifteen, they were in the upper age range of a Secondary Modern school. We had social evenings with them from the youth club, [St Lawrence's Church Youth Group, Mansfield]. ...We used to play the usual games, and dancing, the dancing that was on in the war years, and refreshments, it was just a case of getting to know and talking and making the people welcome. [19]

St Lawrence's Church [Date unknown]

The Interior of St Alban's Church (pre 1968)

St Alban's Church, Forest Town also had a Youth Group and many former members of this, including Thelma Pothecary, have recalled befriending the epileptic children:

> "Some of the children were brought to morning service at St Alban's and one or two eventually joined the Sunday School, so we quickly became aware of them in our community. Someone, (I'm not sure who), suggested it might be a good idea if members of the Youth Fellowship went along to the Home to spend an hour or two with the children playing games – ping pong, draughts, billiards and so on. As we got to know them, we would take our records and we'd all have a little dance. The lads of the fellowship played indoor football with the boys as well, whilst we curled the girls hair and indulged in feminine activities.
>
> From all of this, some real friendships were formed and we were soon asking if we could take the children away from the Home for a walk or for tea at our homes. It was eventually agreed the children with petit mal [a mild form of epilepsy] who were capable of coping themselves when they had an attack, would be able to spend an hour or two away from the Home in our care. So some of us, (with parental approval) had a friend home to tea on Sunday afternoon as long as we had them back again by about 5:00pm.
>
> These children were delightful, and always pleased to see us when we arrived for our games evenings. Everything was properly controlled by the staff, and despite the freedom to have children in our homes and so on, we were not encouraged to wander in and out of the Home on any old occasion. The rules had to be followed."[20]

Audrey Todd remembers that some of them at church were given instruction on how to react if any one suffered a fit during the service. There have been many similar memories, which illustrate how important both sharing and caring was for everyone at that time.

Being a carer was how one local Girl Guide/Ranger, Pat Bird earned one of her badges. Pat was a member of St Lawrence's Guides/Rangers under the leadership of Kathleen Haywood.

"There were certain badges we could wear on our sleeves with pride if we'd done the number of sessions you know to qualify, and the particular one that I was doing, the reason I became in touch with them, [epileptic children] it was a child care badge. ...I went to help and used to go there to help with the children in the week after school.

I was made very welcome. ...I often used to pop in, as well as the hours that I did. ... The chief reason that I went for was to learn all about them and everything. ...The people that were in there, the nursing staff that were in there, were excellent...they taught me what epilepsy was, why it affected people, how to deal with any child that I was looking after, playing with or feeding, or anything like that. With big regard and I think about it now and hear it on telly...to always make sure you'd got the tongue out, and to hold them...so they didn't bang themselves, all that sort of thing you know.

When a couple of children did have fits I was a bit frightened, but I mean you don't show it do you especially when you're that age, ...you do what you've been told, ...I felt a bit shook up after, but then you get used to these things you know. ...I wasn't very old myself, but I went for a long time while they were there.

Which, as you can tell I've never forgotten...it stands you in good stead you know, ...I used to do all sorts of things, help to change the children, dress them, put the coats on or feed them, help with feeding if some weren't eating very well. You used to play games to try and get them to eat, you know aeroplane on the spoon, and all this sort of thing I can remember doing this...I used to quite enjoy going and I went for quite some time there. ...Whether because I was younger they put me with younger ones I don't know.

Sometimes I just painted with them like you would do anywhere where children were gathered, ...and the older ones I used to talk to them about guides and things like that you know, because they wanted to know what I was doing there...I found it interesting. ...I had to do, I can't remember exactly, probably three hours a week altogether 'em, but I used to probably do four, two sessions of two hours...and I enjoyed it."[21]

The Lingfield children may have had a disability, but they were not lacking in ability or skill and they were given the opportunity to demonstrate this to the general public. In December 1944 the Mansfield Chronicle Advertiser told its readers:

'SKILL OF EVACUATED CHILDREN

Exhibition at Forest Town

SOME EXCELLENT PAINTINGS

An epileptic colony from Lingfield of about 250 boys and girls was evacuated several months ago to the Miners Hostel at Forest Town, and last Saturday week a number of Mansfield, Mansfield Woodhouse and Forest Town people accepted the invitation to visit it. Nearly 200 boys and girls took part in activities, like other children, such as appearing in a one-act play, giving a performance on a percussion band, keep fit exercises and carol singing. The colony's own Scouts and Guides were useful on the "open day" in directing visitors and pointing out things of interest.

There was a remarkable exhibition of oil paintings and craftwork. Nearly all the paintings were the work of the boys, since the evacuation to Forest Town, and a number of them possess high artistic merit. Painting is a spare time occupation and all the young artists are under 16 years of age.

Several paintings depicted scenes in the local colliery yard. The craft work section varied from Christmas greeting cards and baby baskets to repairing boots. [22]

The Director of Education for Nottinghamshire Mr J.E. Mason was obviously impressed by all he saw and said this showed 'the results of sympathetic, purposeful control and teaching.'[23]

Teaching children with a disability requires a happy atmosphere and the memories of one local lady are that both the children, and the staff were happy. Some staff were obviously employed locally. Annie Taylor from Forest Town was cook at the hostel when the children from Lingfield were there, [and also for the Bevin Boys]. Her daughter Audrey recalls her mum sometimes found catering for the children on special diets a little difficult because of food rationing in force at that time.[24] Despite this it seems the children managed to acquire a liking for the northern diet of fish and chips.[25]

The Medical Superintendent to the Colony, Dr J. Tylor Fox, was with the children during their stay in Forest Town, and on various occasions he was able to thank local people for their hospitality. One Sunday evening there was a visit by a group known as 'The Compass Players,' they performed two plays entertaining both residents and guests at the hostel. This received special thanks from Dr Tylor Fox.[26] In a speech at the exhibition of children's work (mentioned above) he thanked the people of Forest Town and district for their reception of the colony. He said that 'many people believed epilepsy to be incurable, but that was quite untrue. ...The greater percentage went out, and earned their living just like the general population...'[27]

Inevitably the time came when it was safe for the children of the Lingfield Epileptic Colony to return to their former home. On the last Sunday in February a Farewell Service in St Alban's Church marked the occasion.

> 'The Vicar, Reverend D Mortimer, bid God speed to the Colony and hoped that something had been learned as a result of the contact with local life and interests.'[28]

The children returned to Surrey on the following Wednesday.

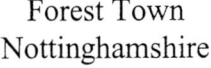

Forest Town
Nottinghamshire

Lingfield
Surrey

Notes

[1]   Forest Town Infants School Log Book 21 July 1939
[2]   Forest Town Infants School Log Book 25 August 1939
[3]   Forest Town School Log Book 14 May 1940
[4]   Forest Town School Log Book has many references to Air Raid warnings
[5]   Forest Town Infants School Log Book 10 May 1940
[6]   Forest Town School Log Book 20 March 1941
[7]   Forest Town Infants School Log Book 20 March 1941
[8]   Turner S *One Hundred Years of St Piers* 1997 pg 50 - 53
[9]   Turner S *One Hundred Years of St Piers* 1997 pg 50 - 53
[10] Monica Palmer
[11] Pat Salmon nee Bird
[12] Mike Parkin
[13] Les Keeling
[14] Mike Parkin
[15] Thelma Pothecary nee Rawlins
[16] Brenda Flinders
[17] Mike Parkin
[18] Les Keeling
[19] Jack Wakefield
[20] Thelma Pothecary nee Rawlins
[21] Pat Salmoln nee Bird
[22] Mansfield Chronicle Advertiser 21 Dec 1944
[23] Mansfield Chronicle Advertiser 21 Dec 1944
[24] Audrey Allott nee Taylor
[25] Turner S *One Hundred Years of St Piers* 1997 pg 50 - 53
[26] Mansfield & Sutton Chronicle 7 December 1944
[27] Mansfield Chronicle Advertiser 21 December 1944
[28] Mansfield Chronicle Advertiser 1 March 1945

No 12 Recruit Course February 1947

Nº 3 POLICE TRAINING CENTRE

By the end of the Second World War the number of serving Police Officers had decreased. In 1942 when they had been allowed to volunteer for the armed forces many would have opted to change their uniform and fight for their country. Additionally, during the years of the war, recruitment for the police service did not take place. This left a manpower shortage at a time when society had to rebuild, and adjust to a life in peacetime Britain.

There was an urgent need to recruit new people to the police force and encourage people to be proud to wear a police uniform and serve their communities. Training courses for the recruits had to be established. Additionally Police Officers, who were being demobilised from the military services, were encouraged to return to their former occupation. These men would need some kind of retraining, as throughout the years of the war, changes had taken place.

The Home Office made plans to establish Police Training Centres and for this purpose the Miners Hostel at Forest Town once again took on a new identity.

The large area of Nissen Huts on Clipstone Road, now became the Nº 3 District Training Centre, and despite being classified as number three, it was in fact the first of the Police Training Centres to open. It was designated to train men from the West Riding of Yorkshire, Derbyshire, Nottinghamshire and Lincolnshire. However, until other training schools were established, the Home Office directed the Chief Constables of Forces including Bedford, Cambridge, Hampshire, Hull, Norwich, Oxford, Reading, Kent, Southampton, Yarmouth, Luton, Sussex and West Suffolk, to send men to train at Forest Town.[1]

Officers to run the Centre were seconded in from other areas. Mr Norman Frost, Chief Constable of Boston was appointed Commandant, and the Deputy Commandant was Superintendent R Roberts from the West Riding of Yorkshire. Initially twelve Instructors were seconded.

Inspectors

Bruton	Doncaster Borough	Allderidge	West Riding
Campsell	West Riding	Tutin	Sheffield City
Mold	Nottinghamshire		

Sergeants

Rhodes	Bradford City	Preston	Lincoln City
Hall	Sheffield City	Swain	Rotherham, Borough
Dangerfield	Chesterfield Borough	Swingler	West Riding (PT Instructor)
Adams	West Riding (Drill Instructor)		

It was intended to increase this number when further applicants could be found.[2]

In the autumn of 1946 everything was being prepared for the new occupants. Staff were being employed to work there. Mr J C Webster was given temporary leave from his job with Mansfield Woodhouse District Council to work for the Home Office as Secretary and Accountant at the hostel.[3] Local girl Monica Palmer, was at that time working as a shorthand typist and bookkeeper in Mansfield.[4] When she heard they were opening a Police Training

Centre and were interviewing people she just went and got a job. The interview took place at the hostel -

> "Mr Webster was there…there was a typewriter, nobody else…Mrs Rollins was a cleaner, I suppose she was a cleaner then, …and she was sending you in and telling you what to do…and I just got the job, and they said, start a week on Monday."[5]

> *So did you actually start before the police came?*

> "Before the police came, and I had to type the lectures, you see, and…they were all typed of course, there were no computers or anything in…'45…Yes, you had to type every lecture and we did 100 copies on the old duplicator, we stencilled them all."

At the end of November 1945 the Police Training Centre was opened, and 73 former Police Officers who had returned from the armed forces began a four-week refresher course. Sir Frank Brook DSO MC HM Inspector of Constabulary (formerly Chief Constable of Nottingham) accompanied by Col T Rawson (Acting Inspector of Constabulary) and Col C H Rawlins (Chief Constable of Derby), officially opened the centre on Tuesday 27th November. Representatives from the press who were at this historic event were told the Forest Town Centre would accommodate 216 students.[6]

Within a short space of time new recruits from various Forces arrived to start a longer course of thirteen weeks. There was mixed reactions to the accommodation:

> "When we arrived there, I must confess our spirits went down a bit. It looked a real gloomy place, as bad as any Army camp…the Nissen Huts were black tarred roofs. There was an area in the front, which later served as a parade ground."[7]

> "It was a bit the same as what I'd been used to really. There wasn't that much difference, naval barracks and what not, ships…it was the same really…in Nissen Huts and rows of beds on both sides…everywhere neat and tidy and painted…just the same as what I'd been used to."[8]

> "It was like going back into the Forces, …a bit more luxurious put it that way. [*laugh*]…it was in Nissen Huts, and you all had your bed, and your bed space, and your cupboard, very similar to an army set up."[9]

A printed report gives the men's sleeping quarters as accommodating six, but it may have varied as there are mixed memories of this. However no-one appears to have forgotten the classrooms were in close proximity to where they slept, possibly because in addition to the beds and lockers, writing tables had also been provided.

> "I know in our room, our section was a central corridor, and you had the sleeping quarters on one side, and the classrooms on the other. So you went straight…from living quarters…into the classrooms."[10]

The Training Centre was well equipped with a reception hall and offices, a dining hall that could seat 250 people, a large hall for concerts or dances, which could hold approximately 400 people. Easy chairs and settees provided for the men's comfort in a lounge, and there was a bar, which served light refreshments including alcohol but not spirits.

The School, from main road

The Assembly Hall

The Lounge

The Bar

The Mess

**Reproduced from 'The Quarterly Journal of the
West Riding of Yorkshire Constabulary April 1946**

The sleeping accommodations and classrooms were divided into four groups and these were known as Atcherley Block, Brook Block, Coke Block, and Egan Block, each named after four of His Majesty's Inspectors of Constabulary.[11] The various paths and roadways around the site were named to reflect the Police Forces in No 3 District:

Lincoln Lane	Wakefield Walk	Sheffield Street
Doncaster Dell	Chesterfield Court	Boston Broadway
Newark Avenue	Rotherham Road	The West Ridings.[12]

The men's uniforms also reflected their different Police Forces:

"...Different Forces, Nottingham City we always thought they were the best; we had those wonderful spiked helmets with a knob on the top of the helmet. Chesterfield Borough had a rather a noted helmet, that was a metal chinstrap, metal round the front of it. Leeds City had a plume on the top of the helmet, more or less like the old-fashioned fireman's helmet. And then people like Notts. County and the odds and sods all had these dull badges and dull tops.

I think Nottingham City were a bit snooty about their uniforms and compared to other Forces it was a magnificent uniform. In those days it was very, very heavy cloth, and of course we had no night uniform there. It was all day uniform which consisted of a tunic...a button up collar, two breast pockets, and two side pockets. ...Your overcoat had two pockets, and it came somewhere between your knee and your ankle in length and fitted in at the waist. I think there were eight buttons on it, all chrome buttons had to get polished. [*laugh*] and of course the helmet that was quite impressive."[13]

The Policemen's helmets could also arouse a bit of fun as remembered by a young painter and decorator working there at that time.

"...little incidents like some folks heads are different sizes so they would joke...a bloke with a little head would put a big hat on, and the bloke with the big head would put a little hat on and they looked very comical with the different size hats and this sort of thing...I mean bobbies were only human and...having a joke, we got to know quite a few of 'em working there like."[14]

Despite the fun and the obvious pride in their own particular uniforms there was no rivalry among the young recruits.

"No none at all. I think there again, the fact that everybody had come from the same sort of background, – straight out of the Forces, you weren't a Yorkshire man, you were a Naval man, or an Army man, or an Airforce man. ...Of course when you come back into civilian life you're just part of the forces...there wasn't any rift between us at all."[15]

On the 19th of November 1945, the first post-war recruit Charlie Walmsley joined the Nottingham City Force, the second was Jack (John) Morgan joining at the beginning of December. Frank Hanford followed him on the 17th of December.[16] Frank recalled that initially they did not have a uniform and used to deliver handbills round some of the Nottingham shops.

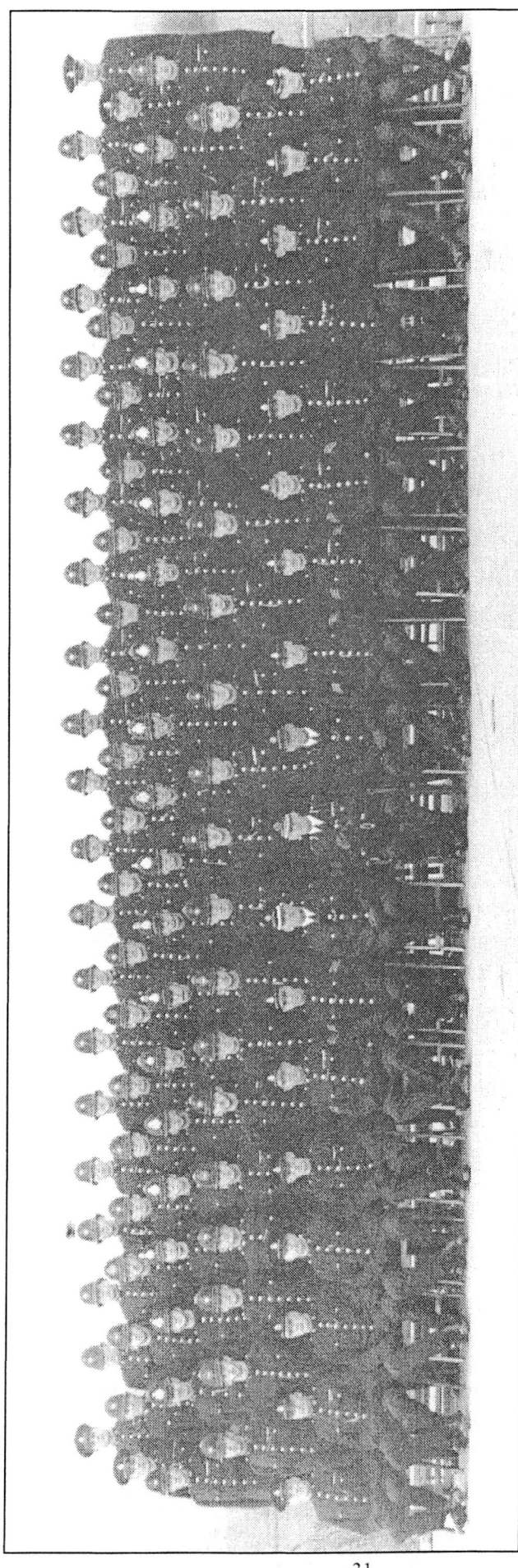

Nᵒ 3 District Police Training Centre
Nᵒ 3 Recruit Course
April 1946

At the beginning of 1946 the three men were sent to the Number 3 District Police Training School at Forest Town, where they discovered just what the training involved.

> "It was three months in total. I went in on the 6th of January and came out on my wife's birthday, the 6th of April. I think there was an exam…at the end of every month. The classes consisted of taking notes, pencil notes at the lecture and at night you had to spend probably two hours, three hours writing them up neatly in a large book."[17]

The note taking from lectures, and the size of the book, approximately A4 size and an inch thick, is well remembered by former policemen. They all recalled there was a tremendous amount of writing to do, and extra notebooks were available for those that filled the first one. The writing was often done in the evening "it was quite a long job so when you'd done your days lectures and you'd got to write it up at night…they thought that by writing, it of course, it was going to sink in deeper. Whether it did or not I'm not sure."[18]

> "We had various people used to come and give us lectures…Doctor Tweedie on first aid; the Chief Inspector Price of Nottingham City, was a ballistics expert. I can't remember whether…we went down to the fire arms department at Nottingham City or he spoke to us there. [Forest Town] Then a pathologist gave us an address, and we went to the forensics science lab in Nottingham."[19]

Dr Tweedie

Doctor Tweedie, and the first aid course are also remembered by both policeman and the staff;

> "We used to call it Doctor Tweedie's Twilight Hour. [laugh] He used to give us a lecture on first aid. A nice chap he was, but there again we'd done all this sort of thing you know in the forces. Everybody had done all this before. It was fairly easy stuff, wounds and that sort of thing."[20]

> "Doctor Tweedie was the Medical Officer of Health…He was a Doctor and had his own practice, but in addition he was the Medical Officer of Health for the police, employed I suppose by the Home Office. …If any of the students were ill or required medical attention we would ring him and get him to come and visit."[21]

Another well remembered person was Drill Instructor, Sergeant Adams who sometimes assisted Doctor Tweedie at the weekly first aid classes.

> "Doctor Tweedie had a very low almost low Irish voice, don't think he was Irish but he'd a very low voice…he could send you to sleep as quick as anything, …of course Sergeant Adams sat on the platform at the side of him and before he came on this particular Tuesday, it was very unusual it was very hot in the February - March of that year for some reason, unbearable in those Nissen Huts, he said 'Last week I saw several men nodding off…the first man to nod off this time goes in front of the Super' …the first man to go to sleep was Sergeant Adams!"[22]

"Everybody liked Sergeant Adams, who was 'a great big fella, rosy faced…ever such a nice fella, the nicest man you could have met in all this world; very unassuming…a great big fella and he used to shout."[23]

It seems he was quite a character; considered to be one of the 'old time coppers', and was known by everybody as 'the Bull', although not to his face.

"He was supposed to take us on a cross-country run and we had disappeared from Forest Town. 'Right, stop, sit on the bank, get your cig'- and he couldn't understand why we hadn't got cigarettes in our pockets. And he handed round cigarettes and we sat and had a smoke. 'Right, we'll get back now. Look tired' and that was him!"[24]

The cross-country runs aiming at keeping the men fit took them down Pump Hollow [at the side of the Training Centre], and followed a countryside route, past Vicar Pond to Old Clipstone, and then returned to Forest Town.

Parades and drill were all part of the weekly routine and while some of the recruits considered:

"Everybody had come out of the Forces, and it really was cushy for the drill sergeant because everybody knew how to do drill at that time. I mean, he had got ready-made drill people."[25]

The secretarial staff, whose office window did not have curtains, overlooked the parade ground, and had a different impression:

"Hoards of men in uniform up and down in front of the office, marching, and they used to come early morning in their P.T kit. It would be bitterly cold and they would stand there right, and it must have been only ten foot, twelve foot, the road that they were on…of course the sergeant always worked from our side so they were all facing in, all looking [at the girls in the office!]."[26]

There was much to keep the police probationers occupied; 'the whole gamut of crime, the legal and other aspects of prevention and detection are covered by the course.'[27]

"It covered quite a large scope, there was a lot to learn. Everybody had a copy of Moriarty, the policeman's bible."[28]

Participating in mock-up road accidents, arresting drunk and disorderly people, visiting local factories, the Fire Station and Mansfield Mortuary, were all part of the course. Sergeant Swingler as PTI is remembered for being in charge of drill and the regular swimming and life-saving classes at either the Mansfield or Sherwood Baths. Great emphasis was placed on swimming and life saving, for which awards were given. In August 1947 the Commandant (Mr R Roberts) said that 'over 2000 swimming awards had been gained by the 1,200 men who had passed through the Centre.'[29] He added that every man had achieved a first aid award.

Life Saving and First Aid Medals won by Pc Martin (Newark Force)

To assist the Police Commandant, and Deputy Commandant in the organising and running of the Centre were civilian staff.

> "At that time the civilian staff consisted of a Lieutenant Colonel Wooding [he superseded Mr Webster], he was in charge of the admin; a Mrs Dover was the house-keeper; a Miss Mitchell was in charge of the sick bay. I can't remember all the office staff, there was a Miss Lynch, Miss Wafflington...Miss Jean Naylor; and one I have remembered for a long while is my wife, Miss Stuart. We met there and married in the May after I came out of the training."[30]

Some of the young women had returned to civilian life after serving in the WRNS or the WRAF and did not have to wear a uniform at the Police Training Centre. One of the girls recalls regularly cycling to work and back on her Hercules bicycle, in a cotton frock and brown leather strap sandals. This is in contrast to the winter of 1947 when;

> "We had two candles on us typewriters to work with, and we worked in our coats and they all wore their coats, all the policemen did, it was so cold, they wore their overcoats...there was no electricity."[31]

There was an open reception with a desk, typewriter and telephone switchboard, one of the push in plug type and the operator had to wear headphones to answer calls.

> "I remember that sometimes if...the head of different Police Forces rang up to make some enquiries I always answered the telephone by saying, "Number three District Police Training Centre, how can I help you."...When they said

Joan Tate

they wanted to speak to the Commandant…I told them to hold, and rang through to the Commandant who said 'keep them talking Joan, …I'll ring you when I can speak to them'…I'd often have long chats with various Police Forces, which was rather interesting…"[32]

Recruit Course Nº 5 July 1946

Working out the men's pay and collecting the wages was another duty of the female staff -

"…it was quite a big job because the wages used to come from each separate Force and so you had all those separately to do up. …I did those…weekly in those days…Mr Frost took me down now and again to the bank. I used to go and collect the money…they were paid in cash…and bring us back in the car, …later on when all these robberies were going on I used to think what a silly thing to do, go at the same time every day and it's anybody that's free drives me down to get it in to Mansfield …I used to come back with this bag of money and I think I once went on the bus…there was no vehicle free…they used to take me down Friday morning, down to the bank in Mansfield, and I had to have the pay ready for them when they came out … at half past twelve."[33]

Memories of the Police recruits pay vary between four pounds and five pounds five shillings [£5.25] The typist received three pounds, and their work could include typing up correspondence, lists for lectures, making tea for visitors such as when the Chief Constables from Rotherham and other areas came. There were occasional conferences and minutes needed typing up:

"Oh and I used to type all the reports, when they'd finished their training after the twelve weeks, I used to go into the committee room and each instructor would come in and then dictate…I'd type it into the typewriter you see. When you think back, it was well done, but I mean when I think back at how we did it."[34]

While the men worked a five day week and could return home if they lived within a reasonable distance, weekends were sometimes left to deal with more sensitive issues as it was sometimes discovered one of the recruits had had a bit of a fling!

"I remember one young lady, they were going to be engaged, and I said I'm sure he's married, she said he isn't, so I looked in his file and he was. …But if anybody, if they got pregnant…I had to go in on a Sunday afternoon. They used to take the statements on a Sunday afternoon, and I had to type them…the girls would turn up at the camp and he'd see them then (Deputy Commandant)…usually on a Sunday, and take a statement and I had to type it Sunday afternoon."[35]

Throughout, the courses appear to have had a set timetable for all the students, and additionally for meal times when a three course meal was served at both 12.30 and 6.30pm for both recruits and staff. These could be a little regimental:

"…every day when we had meals, …one of the Nissen Huts was the dining room, and there was a long table at the top with all the instructors you see…we used to sit about half a dozen at a table…when the Commandant came in he stood up…you sat down when he sat down. When he wanted to leave when he left you all had to stand up. Every day a different person…had to collect the food. …It used to be a bit heavy and I remember one day I'd got a great big tray full of food for half a dozen of us, and he got up to speak, so I had to lean on a table. I thought I'd get it in the neck…and some of the fellas moved so I could just dump it on the table, but it was all very military."[36]

"There was a main hall where we all had our meals and that was quite military. We sort of stood up when the Commandant came in for his meal you know and you had to sit down when he sat down and then when we'd had our meals you could smoke. You couldn't smoke until he told us we could." [37]

"They were quite good meals, there were no two ways about it. They were always a three course meal and plenty of it as well. You had tea in the morning, tea in the afternoon and one after the midday meal…one of the inspectors would stand up towards the end and say 'Gentleman, you may smoke!' There was promptly a big cloud of smoke that went up into the air."[38]

There would have been a number of catering staff at the centre but only two have been specifically recalled and both were named Kathleen. Young Kathleen Palmer was a waitress, working there until she was old enough to train as a telephonist with the post office. Her sister Monica was one of the typists. Another local girl Kathleen Spencer returned home after being in the ATS and found work in the Police Training Centre canteen. Encouraged by the Commandant at the centre, (Norman Frost) she decided to leave and train as a woman police officer at Warrington.[39]

Life at the Training Centre was not all work, there were both leisure and social opportunities, both in and around the locality. Men could participate in table tennis, darts, billiards, chess and cards, or use facilities at the adjacent Forest Town Miners Welfare where the recruits were offered the use of their sports ground, where depending on the season, football, cricket, bowls and tennis were catered for.[40]

There was participation in various competitive events such as a swimming gala at the local Sherwood Colliery Baths in June 1946 when there were inter club events, team races and a polo match. A cross-country event, (June 1946) between recruits at the Centre, was won by Police constable 144 J Wescott, of the Bradford Force, who it seems was a keen harrier and cyclist. Pc 210 [not named] (Notts.) was 2nd and Pc 32 [not named] (Beds) 3rd.[41]

There were sports visits to and from other Police areas. A visit to Rotherham Borough Police in April 1947 needed the competitive spirit when the recruits lost at both football and indoor games. Both policemen and their families, from the West Riding Police Headquarters recreational club, visited the Forest Town Centre in July 1946 for a series of competitive games. When Bradford City Police visited in July 1947 the intention was to play tennis but rain spoiled any chance of this. Two months later in August 1947, it was time for cricket, the visiting team was from No 9 District Police Training College, Cannock, Staffs.

Police musical talent provided local entertainment as Audrey (nee Todd) Swaby who was a member of St Alban's Church at that time, remembers:

> "The man in charge was Inspector Alfred Bruton, who's home was in Doncaster. He had a very good singing voice and trained a Police Choir at the Hostel. During the years after the war, we put on some excellent concerts in the Old Church Hall and Inspector Bruton brought his choir across to help us out. He also did a solo turn and I had the pleasure of accompanying him on the piano."[42]

Some of the men enjoyed a visit to the local pub The Ravensdale, while others preferred to go a little further afield to The Swan, in Mansfield. There was a bar in the Police Training Centre but whether this was open on a regular basis is unknown, however it was open when there were dances and these were a regular feature and are remembered by many people.

> "In the Centre in the dining hall the tables and chairs were cleared and there was a dance there...*were they open to the local people as well?* No it was selective; people knew people that wanted to come to the dance. There was always, nearly sufficient partners for them...it was a three-piece band, I think."[43]

> "They were just like Army dances. Just like service dances...you didn't go back to the old dance halls like before you went in the services. Just like being in another Army, Airforce dance."[44]

> We had dances every month...there used to be a dance...we used to type the invitations and send them to the Shoe Company and the Co-op offices, anywhere else, anywhere where there were a lot of girls we'd send invitations you see...They used to come in droves. They always used to be after invitations from me...we had a band, it was very good.[45]

The village policeman Don Brown and his wife Hilda were also invited to the dances. They would take Don's cousin's daughter Brenda, who was a young teenager at that time, along with them. She really enjoyed the dances.

"I don't know whether they thought I were daughter to Don and Hilda...I used to get asked by one or two, I had one or two dances...waltz, quickstep, foxtrot which I never seemed to get into but waltz's and quicksteps yes I could always do them..."[46]

Reports on Dances and Whist Drives were well reported in the local press, especially when they were associated with the passing out parades of the police recruits.

Mansfield Chronicle 22nd August 1946

POLICE OFF DUTY

A whist drive & dance followed Fridays passing out parade, music being by E Coupe's Dance Band, who played for nearly 400 dancers. For Whist there was 14 tables and winners were Ladies Pc Thwaites (127) Pc Shannon (119) Pc Furness (115) Temp Inspector Campsell won the booby prize with a score of 87. Gents: Pc's Wood (123) Hurry (118) Bentley (115) Pc Cudworth (91) received the booby prize.

Mansfield Chronicle 1st May 1947

FOREST TOWN CELEBRATING

In celebration of the "Passing out" of No 13 course, a dance with music by the Serenaders Dance Band, was held at No 3 District Police Training Centre on Thursday. Over 200 attended, spot waltz prizes were awarded and Inspector Ridley was MC.

Mansfield & North Notts. Advertiser 16 May 1947

FOREST TOWN DANCE

At a dance at the Police Training Centre on Thursday evening last week, music was supplied by the Ambassadors Dance Band, and the spot waltz prizes were won by students. Among those present were the Acting Commandant, Superintendent Roberts, and the Acting Deputy Commandant Inspector Allderidge. On Friday next week the Chief Constable of Lincoln City (Mr H C Walters) will take the salute at the passing out parade of 72 men.

The Passing Out Parade was the climax to weeks of intensive training. Although the courses were of thirteen-week duration, they overlapped. There was a continuation system of both recruitment and training throughout the year. As one class of men was ready to pass out, others were only in their Junior or Intermediate stages.

The Passing Out Parade of the first full course at No 3 Training School was held on the Forest Town Miners' Welfare ground, possibly in March 1946. It would have been a splendid sight. Preceded by the Sheffield City Police Band, two hundred uniformed police officers marched with military precision to the Welfare Sports Ground. Awaiting the parade were local civic dignitaries, Chief Constables from Lincolnshire, Derby, Doncaster, Halifax, Huddersfield, Leeds, Lincoln, Newark, Rotherham, Sheffield, and Chesterfield.

The Chief Inspector of Constabulary Lt. Col Sir Frank Brook, DSO., MC., HM inspected the Parade. Sir Frank was accompanied by the Chief Constable of Nottinghamshire, Lt Col L J Lemon, Mr Philip Allen who represented the Home Office, and Mr Norman Frost the Commandant of the Centre (and Chief Constable of Boston). Ninety men passed out on that first course of post-war policemen trained in the district and it was reported:

> 'The occasion was momentous, for it was the first time in the history of the district that there had been a parade of policemen from so many parts of the country, in addition to many Chief Constables and representatives of Police Authorities.'[47]

**Pc Coy (WRY) receiving the 'Baton of Honour' from Lt.-Col Sir Frank Brook
at the first Passing Out Parade at the Forest Town Welfare Sports Ground**
[From 'The Quarterly Journal of the West Riding of Yorkshire Constabulary July 1946]

Passing Out Parade on the Forest Town Welfare Sports Ground – not dated
[NAO CCNP 35/3/2]

There were many more similar parades and while some of them were reported in the local newspapers as being on the Forest Town Miners Welfare Ground not all are remembered as being there, some recall they were:

> "On the square, in the camp…There was a Chief Constable from…and that was a typical Army passing out sort of parade, everyone in their best bib and tucker and all on their best behaviour all doing all the movements precisely.'[48]

At the final Passing Out Parade to be held at the Forest Town Training Centre, the salute was taken by Mr J Chadwick, the Chief Constable of Huddersfield. A special mention was given to two Nottingham City Policemen, Pc Pollard who had gained the highest marks of the 50 men in No 18 Course and Pc Hughes who was third.[49]

It was not the Passing Out Parade that incurred the newspaper headlines on this occasion. They read:

'Police Training Centre, New Headquarters at Mansfield'[50]

As the last parade took place preparations were already underway to move No 3 Training Centre to a former American Army Hospital on Mansfield Road in Sutton in Ashfield, [now the Kings Mill Hospital].

1947 The Final Recruit Course at Forest Town

Police Constable Ray Pollard recalled:

> "The last week after we'd completed the exams and completed the course, we were all roped in to help move the furniture from Forest Town to Kings Mill…I remember doing probably three or four different trips. Loading lorries up, taking them to the other end, unloading them…"[51]

In the two years the police had occupied the site nearly 1,500 policemen had trained there. Many group photographs were taken, and some like the one on page 42 were signed on the back by all the men, complete with the name of their own particular Force. The houses on Clipstone Road can be seen in the back ground, their tenants would no longer be aware of the 'men in blue,' for the rigorous routine of lectures, drill and parades would not echo around the Forest Town Nissen Huts again.

However the large barrack-like camp on Clipstone Road was not to remain quiet or empty. Within a matter of days there were to be many new occupants as once again the Hostel accommodation was needed for people who were to work in the local coal mines.

No 12 Recruit Course February 1947
Photograph with Recruits Signatures on the back

Notes

[1]   The Quarterly Journal of West Riding of Yorkshire April 1946
[2]   The Quarterly Journal of West Riding of Yorkshire April 1946
[3]   Mansfield Sutton & Kirkby Chronicle 18 April 1946 /The Quarterly Journal of West Riding of Yorkshire April 1946 reports him as being 'until recently on the staff of the Regional Civil Defence Headquarters'
[4]   Monica worked at J H Collins (Manufacturing Chemists)
[5]   Monica Palmer.
[6]   Mansfield Sutton & Kirkby Chronicle 29 November 1945
[7]   Frank Hanford   .
[8]   William Brown
[9]   Ray Pollard
[10]   Ray Pollard
[11]   The Quarterly Journal of West Riding of Yorkshire April 1946
[12]   Mansfield Sutton & Kirkby Chronicle 20 June 1946
[13]   Frank Hanford
[14]   Les Keeling
[15]   William Brown
[16]   Freda Walmsley & Frank Hanford
[17]   Frank Hanford
[18]   William Brown
[19]   Frank Hanford
[20]   William Brown
[21]   Joan Tate
[22]   Frank Hanford
[23]   Monica Palmer
[24]   Frank Hanford
[25]   Frank Hanford
[26]   Molly Hanford nee Stuart
[27]   Mansfield Sutton & Kirkby Chronicle 20 June 1946
[28]   Frank Hanford [Moriarty was the Study Book used for law and all promotional exams]
[29]   Mansfield Sutton & Kirkby Chronicle 14 August 1947
[30]   Frank Hanford
[31]   Monica Palmer
[32]   Joan Tate
[33]   Molly Hanford nee Stuart
[34]   Monica Palmer
[35]   Monica Palmer
[36]   Monica Palmer
[37]   William Brown
[38]   Frank Hanford
[39]   Sheila Baker (her sister)
[40]   West Riding Quarterly Journal April 1946
[41]   Mansfield Chronicle 20 June 1946
[42]   Letter – Audrey Todd March 2002 / This may be the event reported in the Mansfield Sutton & Kirkby Chronicle 17 October 1946
[43]   Frank Hanford
[44]   Molly Hanford neer Stuart
[45]   Monica Palmer
[46]   Brenda Flinders
[47]   West Riding Quarterly Journal July 1946
[48]   Ray Pollard
[49]   Unidentified newspaper cutting
[50]   Unidentified newspaper cutting
[51]   Ray Pollard

Kitchen Staff at Forest Town Hostel

Trainee Miners from the Hostel at Creswell Training Centre

DISPLACED PERSONS

Like the people before them, the new occupants of the Nissen Huts were there because of the aftermath of war. For them it was a war with many different stories, and there were many varied reasons why they could not, or did not want to return to the land where they had once lived. A large number of these people had been sent from place to place, and collectively they became referred to as 'displaced persons.' They were offered the prospect of work and somewhere to live, and for many of them the opportunity to do that began in 1947, in the mining community of Forest Town, Nottinghamshire.

In the area of Nottinghamshire and nearby Derbyshire, the collieries included Mansfield (Crown Farm), Sherwood, Welbeck, Clipstone, Rufford, Thoresby and Creswell. Once under private ownership, this changed in January 1947 when the coal industry was nationalised and they all became part of the National Coal Board, (NCB). It was a time when coal was still in short supply, and there was a desperate need of more people to work in coal mines. The government, anxious to improve this situation, was aware of a 'large number of Poles who had served in their country's armed forces, and did not want to return home after the war.'[1] They were keen to recruit these men, especially any with mining experience, and it was left to the NCB unions to negotiate the terms and conditions for doing this. The agreement, reached in January 1947, said that the local union had to consent to Polish workers being employed at their colliery, that they had to join a union, and in the case of redundancy, they would be the first to go. It is remembered that one local pit would not agree to employing Polish miners:

> "Hence, the Government had a problem with fuel, because there was not enough fuel right so the Government took the Union over the barrel. We have no fuel, either you accept or we send them, so individual pits had a clause they do not accept Poles, Clipstone was one of them…they would not accept foreigners because they cannot work with them."[2]

However the unions of other local pits did agree and this created a need for both training, and an urgent need for accommodation as it was suggested that the men should live within a ten-mile radius of their work. Housing was in short supply and once again the hutted hostels first built for Bevin Boys were considered. When in June 1947 it was said 500 places were needed at Forest Town the police were still occupying these huts. The Home Office agreed to move the police out when they found new premises in Mansfield.[3] This took place at the end of August 1947 and the large encampment was once again referred to as a Miners' Hostel. Over the next few years not just Poles, but people, both men and women of many nationalities and different backgrounds lived, (and worked) at the Hostel. For some the route to Forest Town was via other hostel-type accommodation:

> "Yes, I come 1947 I think it was the June, come from Harrogate transfer to Forest Town." (Gracjan Borrys - Polish)

> "I'm Jozef Wietrzychowski, (Polish) and I used to live in Forest Town Miners' Hostel since '47, 1947…We were supposed to work in Yorkshire. We was in Sheffield Woodhouse, do the training and then supposed to work in the pits in Yorkshire, but the Yorkshire miners gone on strike…We were living in a big camp in Hardwick, [then moved to Abbott Road Hostel]…and then transfer…some from Abbott Road

hostel…Those who work in Ollerton or Thoresby they transfer them to Forest Town."
[November 1947]

"I came to the Hostel '47 about September time…I'd been in different three hostel previously." (Pawel Czarnescki - Ukrainian)

"…was at the Hostel from 1947 till 1949…wife lived at Newark…I was in lodgings at Retford [working as a butcher]…and no chance of a house…Came over the news that they wanted people in the mines, so I thought I'd have a go and that's what happened. I got sent to Sheffield East…some training gallery in a pit there…did so many weeks there training and written examination, and the rest of it. Passed me medical and got set on at Clipstone, which was the nearest place to me where I lived at Newark, and I was put in a hostel." (Lionel George Wortley - English)

"I been born in Poland. I come to England in 1947…I come straight to Yorkshire and stay in Airforce camp for a while…and then from there come to…Forest Town." (Eugen Megdalewitsch. - Polish)

"I was at Forest Town Hostel from 1947…we were staying in hostel in Yorkshire, in various parts of the country before we arrived in Mansfield area." (Josef Jurkiw – Ukrainian)

"Just came into the country…they did say you come to Market Harbro [Harborough] and there seven days and then…where you want to go? assistant canteen?…I don't know it was miners camp so went to here…I went 1947…I was making tea for the residents…and served the staff, meal." (Anna [now Gill] who was then aged 16 – Ukrainian)

"…When I arrived in England first of all we landed in Worksop in a training hostel for a fortnight…then…transferred to Abbott Road Hostel. I lived there for about a year. I landed there in April 1948 and I started work soon after I landed in Abbott Road Hostel. I worked in Welbeck…After a year about 1949 been transferred to Forest Town Hostel because Abbott Road Hostel was closed." (Julian Olexiuk - Ukrainian)

"I arrived from foreign, from hostel…near Edinburgh, in 1948, when I arrived to Mansfield there was two stations." (Siegfried Nawrath, - Polish)

Additionally from the autumn of 1947, and over the ensuing years there were Irish, Latvians, Italians, and various other nationalities at the Forest Town Hostel. The majority were miners but some did have other occupations. There could be upwards of 400 men at any one time staying there. For some it became their home or work place for just a few weeks, unlike others that lived there for years. Some men had already moved from Abbott Road (Mansfield), to be nearer their work. However when the Abbott Road Hostel finally closed in 1949, the occupants were transferred to Forest Town. Some of them were originally Bevin Boys who had opted to stay in the mining industry at the end of the war.

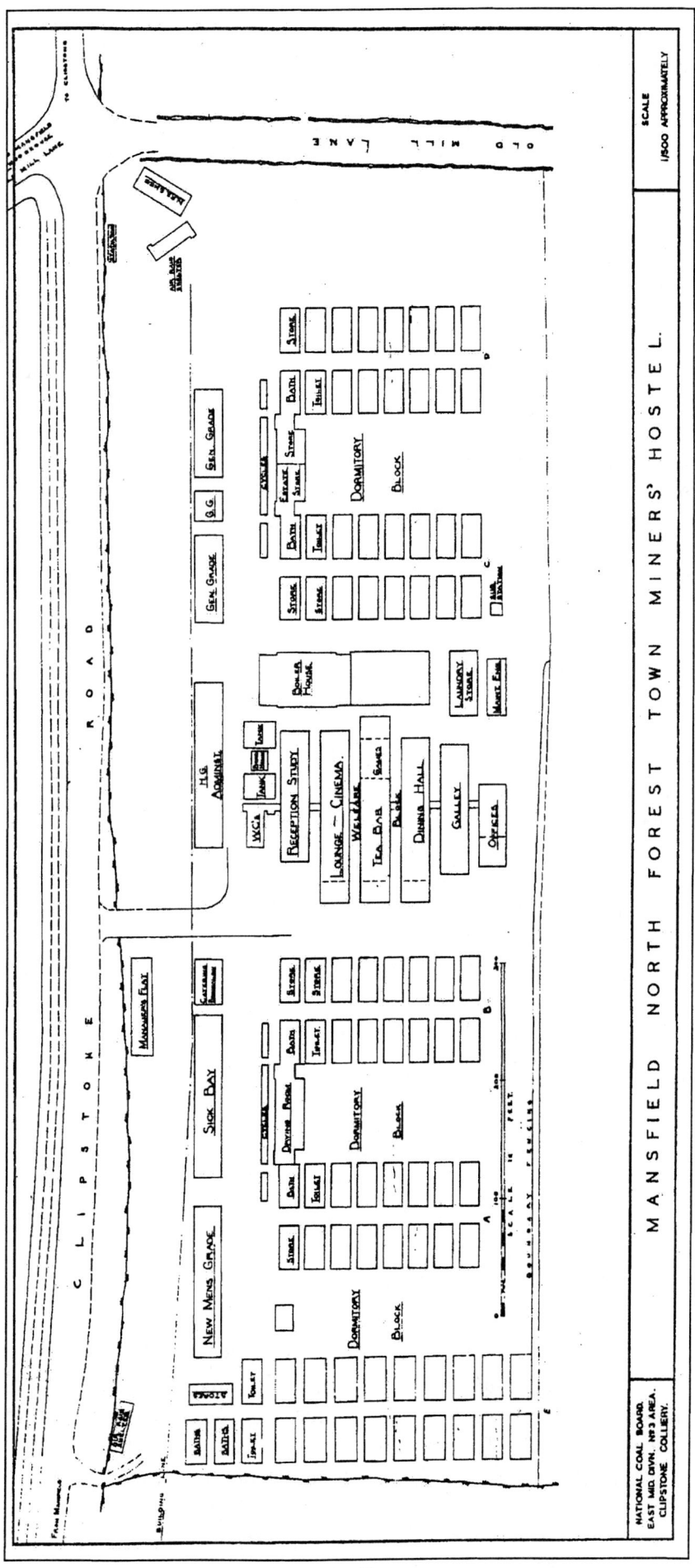

No one appeared to find the Hostel daunting or unsatisfactory, quite the contrary:

> "Soon as I arrived at Forest Town Hostel, I liked the position…was cross-road, church, welfare, shop and…Sherwood garage. There was quite, very pleasant for a site, there was football pitch, cricket pitch…and…felt the right Hostel you know."[4]

> "Well the Hostel looked like any other Hostel really. You know I was quite used to this camp living you know because in the Army we used to stay in barracks."[5]

> "It was very comradeship and very nice. I remember there were approximately one, two, three, about a dozen person per hut. Each of us they had a separate bed and a separate locker. It wasn't too bad. When I say it wasn't too bad…we particularly Ukrainians, I don't know about other nationalities, but we Ukrainians had very hard life in Germany. Therefore when we came to England and we were made very welcome and therefore if you see we did not demand very much. We were thankful for every understanding, for every help…therefore talk about comfort, although there were twelve of us per hut, but to us it was luxury…

> …It was warm because usually there was in some cases there was central heating, but also there was an oven, a stove by you could heat it, …and obviously each member, or every lad who lived in a hut looked after his own bed…to make it look almost like Army type."[6]

Some like Gracjan Borrys remember the specific hut they stayed in – "Hut number eight, in it there was room for twelve people, six at either side, each person had a bed, a locker and a little rug, [the size of a coffee table]". Others recall:

> "The wash hand basins were outside in different place and the toilets were out in a different place, different huts. So there was only the sleeping accommodation which was there, for the miners at that time."[7]

> "Yeah, and there were twelve men, twelve men to a room which er was in winter was very cold and in summer very hot and, er well the impression wasn't too bad. We used to earn five pound a week and the keep used to cost twenty five shillings [£1.25]."[8]

> "The summer time it was quite alright, but the winter time nobody was very happy because it was very cold in the winter. You had a radiator on the corridors, but bedroom dormitory used to be cold, there used to be a 2 inch [50mm] pipe, very cold. Just before I left the camp I buy a motorcycle tyre and fill up with boiling water…you're laughing, but what could you do, you couldn't get a water bottle those day."[9]

Some of the staff lived in, and their accommodation was separate to the workmen's dormitories. Many of them like Marjorie Smith were fortunate to have their own room, which even though it was considered to be 'a bit sparse,' it was a private room and she had the facility to make a hot drink. The incentive of having a room of his own prompted Mr Dunajewski to change his colliery job for that of assistant cook at the Hostel.

"I work first in Blidworth Colliery…I was trying to get a job as electrician, but didn't get it…I started seriously with photography, and to have a room for myself where I could do the printing and the rest, developing, I took a job…as an assistant cook. So I had a room for myself and I could practice my photography."[10]

People like the Manager (Mr Knowles and then Mr Semernic), were far more privileged and lived in his own separate bungalow Siegfried Nawrath,. who was storekeeper at the Hostel for around ten years recalled this and other areas of the Hostel site:

The Main Road into the Hostel

"As you entered…in the centre of the camp was a concrete road, on the right hand side was the Manager's bungalow…he was on his own there…The second, was the catering officer manager…his wife lived with him…and the left hand side, was the housekeeper. From the housekeeper, was the administration where I lived, and behind my hut we had the cleaning ladies…I had a room for myself…but my towels were changed everyday, the beds were made for me, right everything was made done for me and cleaned…the room was very, very tiny, but for a single man you didn't want a big room because only show dust.

From that adjacent to that, was a building with a clock about twenty four inches diameter, and underneath the clock was the toilets, the nearest facility was the toilet. …but on the right hand side, was the general office that was where I work. And my office was behind the boiler house and I had to work half a day down there and half a day here so the Manager could see me, there was no skiving. [laughter] We also had a gardener, …he always come to me if he could have seeds for flowers…the garden on the front it was known for lupins, you could have any colour of lupins you desire in front of that building in the offices. It was magnificent, to look just right and see this flowers."[11]

One or two different gardeners are recalled throughout this period of the Hostel. One is remembered as a Polish man who, because he had been in an accident at sometime in his life, had only one leg. He was said to be called Walter, and after he left a Mr Goddard came from Mansfield and replaced him.

Understandably there are variations on who and what is remembered. People were at the Forest Town Hostel at different times, some were there just a short time while others lived or worked there for a number of years. Likewise they would have no doubt mixed with people from their own background. Additionally there would have been changes to the organisation and running of the premises from 1947 until it closed in 1959.

Throughout all that time the staff and employees were of various nationalities, among them English, Polish, Latvian, Ukrainian, Estonian etc. The memories are of happy times and good comradeship, most people were liked and there was only the occasional adverse comment about a particular person or a brief memory of arguments and trouble. Because some of the Managers had previously been Army or Airforce officers, the Hostel was run with precision and on well-maintained lines.

Mr Knowles was the Manager for a number of years. He was succeeded by Mr. Semernic a Jewish gentleman who is recalled as having a dog named Gamble, who when the office staff had a cup of tea in the afternoon, was always given a saucer of milk.[12]

The Welfare Officer in 1947 was Mr Taylor and later there was a Mr Grayley. While just two accountants have been recalled, Mr Halaran who was Irish, and Mr Mole, another one Mr Grimes, is listed in the 1949 programme on page 58.

Mr Grayley (Left) Mr Mole (Right) and members of the office staff

Over the years, there were different housekeepers, one was Mrs Clarke, also a Miss Smith who went to New Zealand, and then Marian Smith who's sister Marjorie, worked in the offices. When Marian left after two years Mrs. DaSilva became the housekeeper.

With so many occupants the Hostel needed some kind of medical facilities and it was said to have a good sick bay. While the name of the Matron has not been recalled she is remembered as being 'good but strict...she was a nice person.'[13] One lady who is remembered in this capacity obviously worshipped at St Alban's Church just across from the Hostel. In the church magazine, January 1949 Rev. John Spencer wrote:

> 'We do miss Sister Thorne from the Miners Hostel, and wish her good luck in the Name of the Lord in her new sphere at Aylesbury, and may she be very happy in her church life there.'

Another important and necessary job with such a large establishment was that of storekeeper, and it was quite a comprehensive one:

> "I arrived there [1948] and accept a job as a storekeeper...I was in charge of all their material in the Hostel...and me for having the stock...every week, every once a week, right, my office was open. They come with a, with a chit...what I call a requisition...what they wanted for that week so I started week soap, right, powder, all cleaning material, right. Cutlery, pots and so forth and so forth and that's score after issued the new one, replaced them. Then I went with that...to the Manager who discusses I've ordered replacement, right, so the bill was a lot, a lot because, everything was hand wash...The job increased, I was a storekeeper and they made me then cost clerk. So I had to sell...every Friday, tickets to the men for the meals."[14]

There was ample administration and clerical work to do and the office staff and receptionists included Lily Wright and Marjorie Smith. Both these ladies worked there in 1947 for two or three years and then again in the 1950s. They both recalled other girls/young women who they had worked with, Betty Simpson, she came from up north, Maria who was Polish, Sheila White, Honor from Bunny, and Inga a Latvian girl.

Reception Area

"We used to do the books, work on reception, answer the switchboard and they used to have what they call meal tickets."[15]

"I was on the switchboard as well. We used to have to book the men in when they came in and write all their details and everything. Serve them, meal tickets, as well, yes. Give 'em all the post. We also had to take the board at the weekends…we had a little office and sat in there taking their board which they had to pay, I think it was about two pound fifty a week. And then of course all the other things entailed in the office, you know, reckoning up how many meal tickets and so forth and typing I used to do as well."[16]

Meal tickets were well remembered by both staff and residents for with so many people living and working at the Hostel, there were plenty of meals to cater for.

"The meals were provided for breakfast, lunch, cooked breakfast, cooked lunch, if you went to work you could bought for eight pence…sandwiches. The same has been repeated at dinnertime, that's from twelve to one…you could have a whole dinner, you had sandwiches to take to work with you. When you come from work, then you could buy sandwiches in the evening because there was a canteen opened. Because there were two shifts, the cooks worked three shifts. There was a head cook, which must be English because they would not have a foreign man to be in charge."[17]

So there was a canteen? "It was, actually in them days it was very good. I mean we had meals in there because while we were working, and the meals were good. Oh there was nothing wrong with the meals, we had some good cooks in there, most of them was foreign."[18]

Anna was only sixteen when she came to work at the Hostel:

"I had to get up at half past three…half past three in the morning…you had to make tea for the residents to go to work."

And that was everyday, was it? "One day half past three and then the next day half past one until about half past nine…was shift.[19]

What sort of food was it? "Usual cooked breakfast you know, bacon, eggs, sausage…you used to have a packed lunch, you could have cheese, jam or dripping whatever, you know…it was quite good, quite good, I mean considering it was just after the war, I mean everything was still short."[20]

Anna taking a rest from kitchen duties

"You had a book, breakfast and dinner, you had like a little slip, you ripped that off and you come to dining room, pass that over and they give you…breakfast. Then you took breakfast on your tray and you went in dining room, whatever you want was there, cornflakes, bit of bacon, bit of sausages, mushroom and that, and a bit of bread and butter…You could have a cup of tea…same as dinner. It was dinner time from twelve till two and when you were ready you had a ticket, put it there and you take a dinner. That's how it work…but if you want enough [more] you got to forfeit a ticket for a shilling, a dinner ticket and have another dinner if you want."[21]

Kitchen Staff

"…I have to mention, having the meals what we had or had not during the war in Germany, when we came to England and then to Forest Town in particular the meals were rather good. It started with our breakfast obviously and we had our bacon rashers and what have you…there was quite a lot of fish being introduced, ham and eggs and…There was always plentiful of tea and coffee…meal was not too bad. …We were not fussy at that time before we came to England, we were all very hungry, very under nourished, and we were definitely not fussy what we were eating because as the saying goes we felt that we could eat a horse including his horse shoes…"[22]

"…it was a very good canteen. You used to get sausage pie as we called it. The meat that was left over with potatoes and make a pie like…"[23]

"Well I was working as an assistant cook and then I become a cook, nothing special about it, it was just cooking…There were some professional people there, a butcher, there's a pastry cook…I used to produce about 400 dinners. …On Sundays there was crush because everybody come at same hour you see; but in weekday people used to work on shifts so they used to come, the first one 5 o'clock for the 6 o'clock shift. They come half past 4 – 5 o'clock for breakfast and then lunchtime and they come from work at 2 o'clock you know they want their lunch and some come they want their lunch before they go to pit, and so always busy you see…the menu was quite varied. You could have, there was always the roast beef and cottage pies and lot of potatoes. The Irish, the Irish people are very fond of potatoes, I've never seen anyone eating so much potatoes…"

"The best bit was the pudding…there always was pudding, anything what's left from the breakfast, off cuts or broken slices, they used to put on one tray, special on side. Then at dinner used to put in big tray, put some, this raisin, stick the raisin between the custard and potato [?] that was nearly every day."[24]

Did you produce any sandwiches for the miners?

"Yes, they used to do the sandwiches, but you 'ad to pay for them you see. Sandwiches of cheese, ham, or beetroot. They didn't like very much ham because when you get ham down the pit you know it gets watery. [laughter] Cheese was the best."[25]

"…they ask you wants snap, you give them what they ask…you give them jam or cheese that's all they want jam and cheese, jam and cheese that's all."[26]

Sandwiches have definitely stayed in people's memories. Jozef Wietrzychowski said for him it was mostly bread and jam, supplemented by a big bottle of water to drink down the pit, where it could be very warm and thirsty work. Others like the office staff who could eat in a rather different environment were occasionally a little bemused by their sandwiches:

"We had two Polish men come to work in the office…well we had one first, his name was Vivolitz…I remember him because he said 'I'm going to fetch some sandwiches, do you all want one?'…for when we're having coffee. I said 'yes please', he come back with cheese and jam on same [sandwich]!…I said 'my goodness you don't expect me to eat that'…he said 'it's lovely'. We all eat it 'cause we were hungry you see, we were ready for a sandwich but we hadn't time to go down and fetch anything."[27]

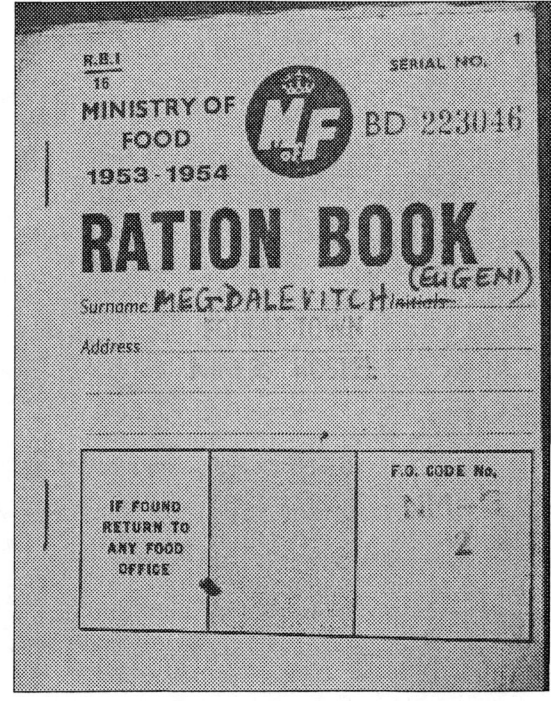

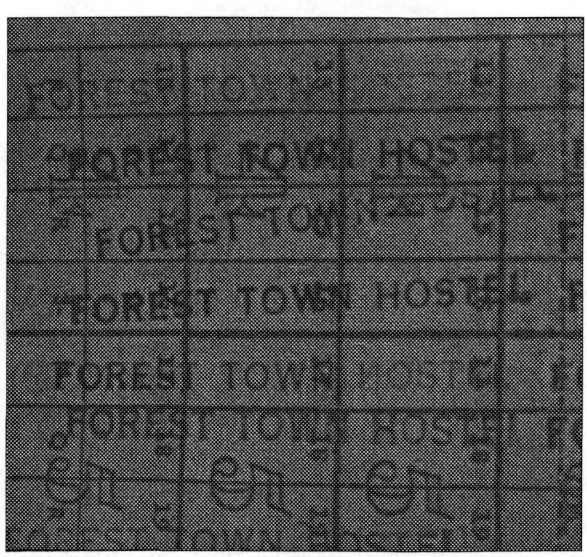

A Hostel Resident's Ration Book

Time was important, especially for the men on an early shift and to ensure they were not late for work the Hostel had a system for waking them:

> "The man, the watchman, he had all numbers. You used to tell him which number what time to wake up, and he used to come round and wake you up."[28]

> "There was a night watchman on...watchman would come and give me a tap on the shoulder at about five in the morning to get up and have an early breakfast."[29]

There are other memories of the shift system:

> "...usually though there's men on three shift...they got to go to work and one special name was Peter, who was cowboy he didn't go to work, a lot of people were on the afternoon shift and day shift, night shift. Unfortunately I was night shift and I sometimes only had two hours sleep, because the cleaner would come, somebody else come and bang this door, bang this something else, I wake up that's it, couldn't sleep any more."[30]

With so many occupants the cleanliness of the Hostel was important and it is to the credit of everyone that it is remembered for being so clean, even if they did occasionally wake someone up.

> "The girl, cleaning ladies there was six, from the Forest Town, altogether we had about twenty, or over twenty because that depends how big the number of the Hostel, were allowed to have staff. That was the number, we had to send a return for the staff, then we were allowed to have the staff in."[31]

The men who worked at Mansfield (Crown Farm) Colliery would be able to walk to work but for those working at other more distant collieries buses were laid on:

> "We had a Blidworth bus, and Bilsthorpe had their own bus you see. [Number] 108 Blidworth, it used to come from town come to Forest Town, and take one or two more in Forest Town, it would turn around and come to Hostel and take from there, and when we got to Blidworth of course we were full, ...quite a lot workers from Hostel in Blidworth."[32]

Did it actually come in the camp or did you wait for them on the main road?

> "We wait on a Hostel gate, we waiting there for a bus...and it come from Forest Town and stop agen gate, and only there for a few minutes...if anybody late can you hold up a minute, so and so has got to come...I think the bus fares was one and sixpence [7½p] for return."[33]

Travelling on the bus was often quite a memorable experience for some of the young men who were in their late teens or early twenties. The journey took them past a Women's Land Army Hostel in Old Clipstone, where there would sometimes be lines of underwear hanging out to dry, this encouraged a bit of friendly shouting from male occupants of the bus.[34]

For the men at the Forest Town Hostel a laundry service was available, and while some recall a laundry on the site, where people did their pit clothes others have memories of personal clothing being sent every week to a Laundry in Mansfield. They liked to have fresh clean clothes for their periods of relaxation. This may just have been in the Hostel, where they sometimes had film shows or elsewhere.

> "On Saturday nights we used to go to pictures in Mansfield, Granada or Grand or whatever. Also we used to go to dances in Nottingham. In Mansfield there were Palais de Dance on Saturday, and then on Sunday we could dance in Hostel, but pictures we used to go on Saturday."[35]

The dances at the Hostel were popular, and the memories of the music and swirling dance skirts have remained with some of the local girls who met their future husbands at these events. It seems girls often came from quite a distance to attend the dances:

> "...Used to be dance day you know...girls come from Hucknall, Woodhouse, Mansfield, you know sometime they weren't supposed to because they had to go home. After 11 o'clock they go home because it was last bus...but them people them girls from Woodhouse they used to go across Old Mill, New Mill Lane cross on the foot...so cause this man, no matter which nationality he was to escort them sometimes, you know across the fields..."[36]

> "Then of course on Sunday nights they had dancing and everything, and a lot of people and girls from Forest Town came, a lot of them married Poles including myself. [Lily married Max Kurnatowski – chairman of the social committee]...my parents used to go, they went, on a Sunday night, 'cause I used to go you see, and that was before I actually started going out with Max."[37]

> "Oh yes there was dances, organised dances because they used to organise a Polish band, you know people who work in pit, but they got together and organised a band and they used to play. There was a big hall...and they had a dance Saturday."[38]

There were some very memorable and colourful events held at the Forest Town Hostel, with people in national costume.

The Hall where dances and other memorable events took place

"Well quite often they used to organise culture exhibitions and every nationality used to put their[s] on. They used to dress like boys and girls in national costume, and we had wonderful Easter eggs and other embroidery, towels or whatever, you know our traditional, same as we have it. Of course I remember there were Polish, Latvian and Lithuanian, the four nationalities that were the most active Latvian, Lithuanian, Polish and Ukrainians in those days yes."[39]

"There was exhibition all nationality...in the Hostel itself...other people used to come from outside to look...*So what was in the exhibition?* The national costume...[wife speaking 'beautiful']...There was one day...that time they have exhibition, national, you know exhibition there was Polish flag, Ukrainian flag, Latvian, it was, ah, there was lots."[40]

"...and on the first year it was opened, we had like an, I'd call it an anniversary. I don't know, I can remember, I think it was a dance, ...we had this gorgeous big cake and it was like a pirate box, ...it had a lid on it...and then it had flowers in it, I remember that ever so well and it was beautiful this great big cake we had. Yes for the first anniversary."[41]

The Second Anniversary in 1949
was also a time of festive celebrations as this programme shows

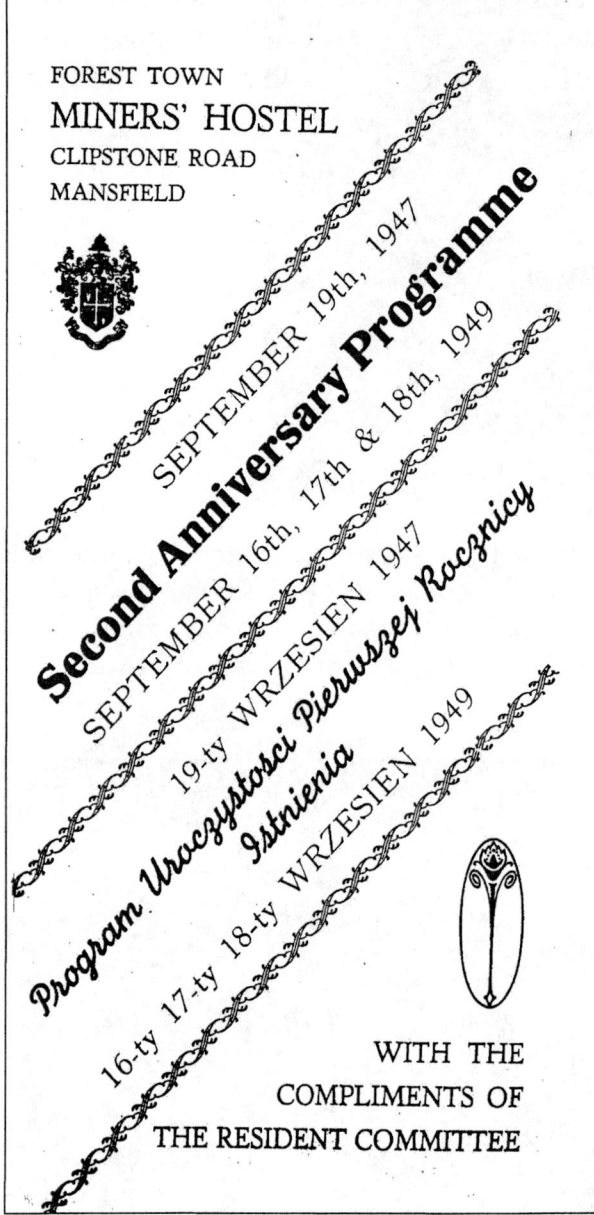

FOREST TOWN
MINERS' HOSTEL
CLIPSTONE ROAD
MANSFIELD

Second Anniversary Programme

SEPTEMBER 19th, 1947

SEPTEMBER 16th, 17th & 18th, 1949

Program Uroczystosci Pierwszej Rocznicy

19-ty WRZESIEN 1947

Istnienia

16-ty 17-ty 18-ty WRZESIEN 1949

WITH THE
COMPLIMENTS OF
THE RESIDENT COMMITTEE

Executive Staff

Manager	...	MR. G. W. KNOWLES.
Accounts Officer	...	MR. R. W. GRIMES.
Caterer	...	MISS M. SLEDMORE.
Equipment Officer	...	MR. F. G. E. SPURR.
Housekeeper ...	...	MRS. M. A. DASILVA.
Welfare Officer	...	MR. S. TAYLOR.
Sister	...	MISS K. M. TEMPLETON.

Residents Committee

Chairman :
B. SMIEJKOWSKI.

Members :
M. LEWANDOWSKI
A. PIETRASZEK
W. JAKEL
A. WILKUS
W. SPODZIEJA
J. MARKHAM
I. MURNIEKS
N. MARKULIS
T. BURYJ
W. STASIW.

Appreciation

The Regional Controller, North Midland Region, The Manager and Executive Staff, wish to express their thanks to all Residents and Staff who have contributed so willingly towards making this Second Birthday Celebration such a great success.

1949 Birthday Programme.

Friday, 16th September:

7 p.m.   Cinema Show.
SID FIELD & GRETA GYNT
in
London Town
in Glorious Technicolor,
also COMEDY, CARTOON & SHORTS.

Saturday, 17th September:

DISPLAY OF NATIONAL FLAGS.

3 p.m.   International Art Exhibition
in the Games Room.
To be Opened by the Regional Controller
MRS. M. FORD.

3.30 p.m.   Football Match.
Forest Town Hostel v. Abbott Road Hostel.

4 p.m.   Volley Ball Competition
between
Forest Town, Abbott Road, Edwinstowe,
Hardwick and Alfreton Hostels.

Saturday, 24th September:

6.30 p.m.   Polish Theatre & Ballet
Saturday,   (ZESPOT POLSKI BALET)
September 17th: in the Lounge.

7.30 to 11 p.m. DANCE.
POLISH DANCE ORCHESTRA.
NOVELTY PRIZES.

Sunday, 18th September:

INTERNATIONAL DAY.
LARGE DISPLAY OF NATIONAL FLAGS.

10 a.m.   Catholic Service
will be held in the Study.

10 a.m.   International Art Exhibition
will again be Open in the Games Room.

2.30 p.m.   Table Tennis Match
in the Lounge.
Forest Town Hostel v. Hardwick Hostel.

3 p.m.   Tug of War.

3.30 p.m.   Classic Records.

4.30 p.m.   HIGH TEA.
Menu.
Cold Ham and Tongue
Russian Salad
Mayonnaise
—o—
Fresh Fruit Salad
Ice Cream
—o—
Brown and White Bread
Rolls
Butter
—o—
Birthday Cake

7.30 to 11 p.m.
CARNIVAL DANCE.
BERNARD HARRISON AND
FULL ORCHESTRA.
PARADE OF NATIONAL COSTUMES
AND FLAGS.
MALE CHOIR.
SPOT WALTZ & SPECIAL PRIZES.
COLOURED & SPOT LIGHTING.

Christmas was recalled in various ways. The Hostel was decorated and there was always a Christmas tree. Some of the office staff had an enjoyable time when they volunteered to work, and after serving the residents they sat down to eat with them. The meal was a traditional Christmas one produced in the days of food rationing. The Ukrainian Christmas falls on 7th of January and in 1948 this was celebrated with a dinner at the Horse & Jockey in Mansfield, it was at that festive dinner that some of the

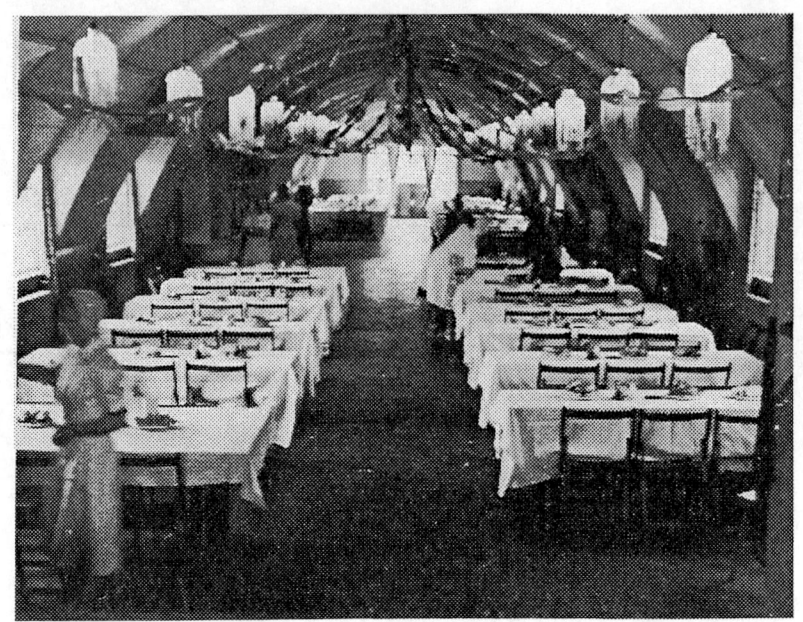

The Dining Hall

Ukrainians tasted their first Christmas Pudding. The guests included Mr Knowles, the Hostel Manager, and Councillor Mrs Smedley from Forest Town. In the years following, various different halls were hired for the Christmas celebrations, and the ladies would do the catering by preparing the food at home first.

When the hostel opened in 1947 there was no Catholic Church in Forest Town, however it seems one good lady did attempt to encourage the newcomers to attend a church:

> "Oh there was invasion, oh I remember there was, soon we landed Forest Town there was this lady come there from different denomination, trying to convert us to Baptist Church and Salvation Army or I don't know! …"[42]

Occasionally a priest visited the Hostel to take Mass, but on most occasions people would go to St Philip Neri's Church in Mansfield or a Catholic Church in Nottingham.

Mr Dunajewski has not forgotten that religion played a minor part in stopping a game of football in the village:

> "There used to be a football ground behind the church, and we played one Sunday a match and the priest come flying 'stop playing on God's day' [laughter]…we did not know we were not to play on Sunday."

Football was something that many residents enjoyed and before the houses [Tudor Avenue, Coronation Drive etc] were built, a field below the Hostel was used for football. They had organised matches with Polish teams from other areas including Nottingham and Sheffield. There were some very enthusiastic and good players who helped the local team win prizes.

One of the Hostel Football Teams on the field below the Nissen Huts
Forest Town Miners' Welfare building can be seen in the background.

Netball and volleyball were also popular games that were played with the different nationalities making up teams and playing friendly matches at the Hostel. Additionally there were memories of a Ukrainian and Polish ping-pong competition. Some of the men used the gymnasium facilities that had been left when the Police Training School moved elsewhere, and there were also boxing matches.

"There was an Irish fellow, who lived in the Hostel and the National Coal Board of Berry Hill they had boxing matches, and he used to box and he was very good at it."[43]

For those who preferred something a little less strenuous there was a snooker table, or even a game of cards. However no gambling was allowed, and it seems the men found it hard to play cards for matchsticks not money, so they played out of the way of the welfare officer. This was often on Gracjan Borrys' bed as it was near a window and a quick escape could take place if it was needed.

Volleyball Game

Understandably the Hostel did have some rules, the men were not allowed to have women in their rooms and no alcohol was allowed.

"No there was no alcohol in Hostel no no, I remember one chap he start to make his own brew, but...it was no long before they discovered him so Manager gave him marching order."[44]

It is doubtful if the police were needed for that incident but they did frequently visit the Hostel, checking on new residents and the numbers in the hostel:

"You see but the police, very, very crafty, they come every morning, and take [look at] ...all the entry books, all the newly arrival per week...sat sometime on my desk all morning, ticking all the entrants of the arrival, which we have to provide them. But of course, as the police got very tight lip, ...you only say yes or no, that's what was the answer, you say yes or no. ...You had to tell him what he wanted to know...but he only say yes or no...The policeman live in Forest Town, and there was a little house there...this home and his office."[45]

"Oh yes, we had a policeman, in Hostel...he used to come to Hostel...normally afternoon and evening, go and have a cup of tea and all that, and chatted to watchman and his mate. ...Anyway when office open during the day we just going through files looking who come, who left and this sort of thing."[46]

It seems that it was easier to write the name Pole, than to spell the other nationalities, like Ukraine, Estonian etc. Therefore many people were written down under the heading of Polish rather than their correct ethnic group. So it is not surprising that many people still refer to the Hostel as the Polish camp.

"...they were mixed up with the Poles, and the police when they comes, they only knew one name, Poles. Chad [local newspaper] in Mansfield only knew one name, Poles because they couldn't flipping spell it. They couldn't spell the other nationality, ...they didn't know their geography on the continent. Because, and the police say how do you spell Czechoslovakian they takes me half an hour just to spell it, might as well put Poles."[47]

From 1947, when people of so many different nationalities stayed at the Hostel many of them had to overcome the problem of language and communication.

"I d'int speak not a word! ...If you talking to me I just say Ye Ye Good Morning, Good Night that's all I know when I have to pick in six month the language." (Anna G.– Ukrainian)

"...the main language there were, the Ukrainian, the Latvian, if they were talking to each other very careful they would understood each other...similar language, you see, ...everybody wanted to learn English, right, so they spoke English. It broken, they tried to understand because by speaking you learn...The Army before you was, before you were demobbed, they provide you with...a course of English, ...your basic English, you see, and the rest...you have to pick it yourself. That was the only I would say disadvantage for any foreigner, ...of course you...always pick up, the bad ones first. ...You get a red face because you think oh I can speak English, what do you do you bring a bad word, and it start people laughing, they're walking out on you. So, in your own way, you learn that you are saying something that you shouldn't, then of course the young ladies come to you and say you shouldn't be saying that, that is very bad word, right."(Siegfried N.– Polish)

"I can remember…when the displaced persons started coming, Poles, Ukraines whatever and I also worked there…you know we painted a hut at a time, they'd move out, we'd go in and do the decorating. …We did get to know quite a few of the people, but I couldn't tell you any of their names like because these Polish names…you can't remember 'em can you. …The first English they taught 'em at pit were all the swear words…they learnt to swear before any other English like you see so they could communicate to you like…I think it were done deliberately sort of thing, you know…"(Les K. – English)

"We started learning English in Egypt, while training as a radio operator there…we always used to have er English liaison officers…and then I used to be in the Army. I spent most time in south of England, and we used to have lessons in English, and when I came to Mansfield I couldn't understand anybody, what they say."(E.Dunajewski. – Polish)

"We came we could not speak practically at all in English. Whilst we were staying in hostel in Yorkshire…we did have to take a crash course in English; when I say a crash course, we were taught a floor, a ceiling, a window, a table, a chair, indeed only words, but then we started putting words together, and tried to make sentences. …Because we were young at that time and to learn English language it came more or less easily for us. …"(Josef J. – Ukrainian)

"…We didn't really have any problems and we had a Polish girl in the office any way if we did for the Polish language…cause we had a lot of English speaking people in there as well, you know. …Once they all have a number on their meal ticket, they all had a number, so when they come for the mail I'd think of the number and I'd know who it was. …Eventually you get to know all the names as everyday they come for the mail, or they come and talk to you, or come and ask you for something, eventually you remember and for years I could remember all the names and the numbers."(Lily K.– English)

Office Staff

Not surprisingly over those years both romance and tragedy prevailed. Some residents met and married people of their own culture, while a number of local girls married people from the Hostel. They met at social events such as the dances or because of their work situation.

"I sort of knew him…he was chairman of the committee…he used to ask me to do some typing. I wouldn't do it for him very often because I was always busy, I said let Maria Cheeba, she was a Polish girl in the office…so I used to say you do his typing for him. Then one night we met at the bus stop, you know, and I was with the housekeeper…Marion Smith, sister to Marjorie Smith, he asked me to go out with him…I said oh no I can't I've got to get home I'm tired. He said would you go out with me on Saturday so said I don't know…he said to me do you want a cigarette, I said no I don't smoke in the street, he said well just take one. Well it was a Woodbine…and from that day on she [the housekeeper] called me Mrs Woodbine, she said you'll marry him…Seven weeks after I started going out with him, he asked me to marry him and I said yes and we got married in the following March." [48]

Max & Lily on their wedding day

Marjorie Archer was another young woman who worked at the Hostel. She also married a Pole, someone who her friends recall as being a real gentleman. Sadly when Marjorie went on her first visit to Poland she was killed in an accident. There are also memories of people being rejected by someone they fell in love with and as a result took their own life.

For one Polish father and son, the joy of being reunited was soon ended when a pit accident at Bilsthorpe colliery in May 1948, took the life of the son, 21 year old Zbrigniew Wolk. The younger man was a resident at the Forest Town Hostel while his father was living at Winter Camp near Goldalming, and a local newspaper told of how they had only been reunited the previous Easter after being separated.

'Mr. A. Homes, Manager of Bilsthorpe Colliery, said "I express sincere sympathy with the relatives of the deceased. The father is with us, and I would like him especially to convey this expression to the mother, sisters and brothers of the deceased boy. The sadness of this case is rather intensified when we know that the family have been separated for so long. The father and son have been separated for a long time, wandering about different countries of Europe, and only recently did the father and boy make contact. I think the sadness of this is intensified by the fact that they have only just been re-united and this accident happened."

Mr. Payton [occupation unknown] joined in the expression of sympathy. He was very pleased to say that the youth had had a proper training and Mr. Walker, the deputy, had stated that he was always satisfied with the way the boy had carried out his duties. Several reports had been received about Poles, which definitely told them that those men were doing a splendid job in our mines. He believed some had had previous experience in mines. At any rate they were doing a useful job in this country, and they were very sorry to lose any of them.'[49]

A very sad occasion.
The funeral of Zbrigniew Wolk, at Mansfield Cemetery

However there were more happy memories than sad ones, and just the occasional scandal when a local shopkeeper ran off with someone from the Hostel. Nonetheless local traders benefitted from the Hostel residents custom. In 1947 the nearest public house was the Ravensdale and in December 1952 when the Prince Charles opened people had the option to go there. Names of local shopkeepers are recalled; Mr Bingley, Mrs Cupit, Madge Hare, Mrs White. What the shops sold is additionally remembered.

"I think Forest Town community never had a problem in Hostel...used to go to fish shop...the post office also, just below garage, Sherwood Hall garage, that paper shop, used to bring paper, newspaper in a morning to Hostel. ...Another shop was on a Ellesmere Road, just behind the garage...he used to make good business, he used to get some food from Ireland...he used to have salami and pickled herrings...pickled onions." (Pawel C.)

E. & M. BINGLEY
FOR
GROCERIES & PROVISIONS

HIGH-CLASS FRUIT
& CONFECTIONERY

ELLESMERE ROAD, FOREST TOWN
Telephone :: Mansfield 5052

From 1953 Coronation Festivities Programme

"...distinctly remember the Poles...They used to use the newsagents again for a source of food supply, the shop at that time being taken over by Tom and Madge Hares and Mr Hares...brought in the sort of food from Eastern Europe that appealed to the Poles and probably the Ukrainians as well...you'd go in and you'd see all the salami, all these sausages hung up, jars of gherkins..." (Mike P.)

"After a while there were a regular van with continental stuff come…he used to park just outside the premises of the Hostel, and he used to sell various continental stuff like belly pork as it is called now, like salamis and such like. …Therefore those lads that bought some of that food and then wanted to substantiate their own jam for example they used to take that down pit. Some of the salami was sort of quite mildish, others it contained quite a lot of garlic. …Can you imagine any person going down pit with the snap full of salami that smelled rather strongish of garlic, and there is only one way that there was ventilation going only one way down pit…and so whole pit used to smell. Obviously there were various opinions about it." (Josef J)

From September 1947 until well into the 1950s there were people of many nationalities living in the Nissen Huts at Forest Town, knowledge of this has been gained from people's memories and newspapers. Old documents just give statistics. In 1948/49 the capacity was for 600 residents, while in 1950/51 it is given as 816, indicating additional huts were added at some time. However from the figures quoted it was never completely full.[50]

The residents moved out when they obtained a house to rent or buy. Some took colleagues with them, renting out spare rooms to help with their own finances. For some people this did mean they could be together as a family again. While working at the local pits had often provided a regular wage, for some men it had meant leaving a wife and family in Skegness, Doncaster, Newark and elsewhere.

The Forest Town Hostel had for the many people who had stayed there, provided a substantial place to live. It is still remembered today for its good atmosphere, cleanliness, social life and "…at weekend you noticed the recreation hall, there was the fresh flowers cut in vases."[51]

**Ukrainians from Forest Town Hostel at their first Christmas party
January 1947 in the Horse & Jockey, Mansfield**

Choral Entertainment [Date Unknown]

Notes

1. W Ashworth *The History of the British Coal Industry Vol 5 pg 152*
2. Siegfried Nawrath
3. PRO LAB 26/196
4. Pawel Czarnescki
5. E. Dunajewski
6. Josef Jurkiw
7. Siegfried Nawrath
8. E. Dunajewski
9. Eugen Megdalewitsch
10. E. Dunajewski
11. Siegfried Nawrath
12. Marjorie Smith
13. Lily Kent
14. Siegfried Nawrath
15. Marjorie Smith
16. Lily Kent
17. Siegfried Nawrath
18. Lily Kent
19. Anna Gill
20. George Wortley
21. Eugen Megdalewitsch
22. Josef Jurkiw
23. Jozef Wietrzychowski
24. Gracjan Borrys
25. E. Dunajeweski
26. Anna Gill
27. Lily Kent
28. Jozef Wietrzychowski
29. George Wortley
30. Gracjan Borrys
31. Siegfried Nawrath
32. Eugen Megdalewitsch
33. Eugen Megdalewitsch
34. Gracjan Borrys
35. Julian Olexiuk
36. Gracjan Borrys
37. Lily Kent
38. Jozef Wietrzychowski
39. Julian Olexiuk
40. Pawel Czarnescki
41. Lily Kent
42. Gracjan Borrys
43. Siegfried Nawrath
44. Gracjan Borrys
45. Siegfried Nawrath
46. Eugen Megdalewitsch
47. Siegfried Nawrath
48. Lily Kent
49. Mansfield Chronicle Advertiser 14 May 1948 Inquest Report
50. PRO LAB 22/63
51. Pawel Czarnescki

HUNGARIAN REFUGEES

At the end of 1956 the Forest Town Hostel welcomed a new group of people to stay in its accommodation. Like others before them, they were there because of trouble and turmoil in their own country. These new people were refugees from Hungary who needed somewhere to live and to work, and they had been encouraged to come to the Mansfield area to work in the local coal mines.

There had been a continuing shortage of coal miners since the war, and despite the industry having recruited many Poles, Ukrainians, Latvian, Italians etc. this had not been fulfilled. There was still 9000 men needed, especially in the expanding coalfields of Yorkshire, the East and West Midlands and parts of South Wales. After the Hungarian uprising in 1956 many people took refuge in camps on the Austrian Border. Representatives from the Coal Board and National Union of Miners went to visit the camps. In January 1957 Mr James Bowman, Chairman of the National Coal Board, gave an interview to the Press Association where he told them:

> "They went to camps on the borders and found that there were miners and other fit young men ready and anxious to start a new life in the pits of this country. When we got our teams report, we at once decided to bring some of these men over. This would not only be in the name of humanity but would help us get more coal. As in years past, we hope this year to recruit about 60,000 British workers, and if we can get four or five thousand Hungarians as well, it will really help."[1]

When this interview took place the Hungarians had already started to arrive in Forest Town. On the 29th November the Chronicle Advertiser told readers that 'Seventy Four of the many thousands of refugees pouring out of Hungary arrived in Mansfield on Saturday'. A photograph of these young men in their teens and early twenties accompanied the report and it told of how they would be staying indefinitely at the Forest Town Hostel.

The men were welcomed to Forest Town by the Vicar of St Alban's Church, Rev Philip Walker. He told the men that the village now had a Catholic Church and the times of the services. For some men, knowing they could attend Mass would be important. News of the men's plight had obviously reached the community beforehand as Church members had collected items of clothing to help them. Very few of them spoke English and they were fearful of giving their names because of reprisals to any family members that had been left behind.

Rev Philip Walker

The Parish Hall (An early view)

On their first Sunday evening in Forest Town refreshments and social activities were laid on for the men in the Parish Hall. This gave them the opportunity to meet with local people and taste a bit of home baking done by ladies of the church.

During the following week four more groups of Hungarian refugees arrived at the Forest Town Hostel making a total of 200, and as the Hostel still had other occupants it was now classed as full. An appeal was made by the manager of the Mansfield Labour Exchange for householders with rooms to spare to take men in as lodgers. Not all of the men had volunteered to work in the coal mines, some of those with a skilled trade had quickly obtained employment and could support themselves.[2]

With so many Hungarians moving into the area the East Midland Division of the National Coal Board decided to expand the existing hostel accommodation at both Forest Town and Alfreton and to re-open facilities in Hucknall. At Forest Town additional wooden huts 38 x 19 were to be added and the appropriate furniture and bedding purchased. While some of the other facilities were felt to be adequate, the building of a separate dining room for the staff would release dining space in the main dining room for the residents. The cost of this new accommodation and furnishings was in the region of £38,000. It was authorised in February 1957 and was required around Easter. [3]

By this time there were many Hungarians staying at the Hostel, discovering what the local area was like and what it would entail if they were to work in the collieries around the Mansfield region. One of the essential things for them to learn was the language. For the men who had signed an agreement to work in the pits, attending English classes was part of their training for which they would be paid the surface minimum rate.[4] The local newspaper reported that the first Hungarians at the Forest Town Hostel were being taught English by a Polish lady in the Ravensdale Day Release Centre,[5] however it seems a classroom was soon provided at the Hostel itself.

Charles Dery was 23 when he came to this country. He and colleagues landed at Heathrow in December 1956. They were first taken to a refurbished Army camp in Wiltshire, and between Christmas and New Year they were moved to Brigg in Lincolnshire. The accommodation this time was the site of an old chicken farm. However by mid January they were moved to Forest

Town where the new Hostel was regarded as being an improvement on the previous two places.

> "And well that's where we settled in and I believe somewhere around the end of January we started school...classrooms...in the Hostel, all those that had signed on to work down the coal mines round the area, started learning basic English.
>
> There was just the one English teacher, we were only learning the language, there were...I believe some mathematics as well, so there were just the two....I believe one was a Polish lady who lived in Layton Avenue...and gentleman, I can't remember his name, but he only came in occasionally to teach us basic mathematics, which the mathematics are the same in every language as far as I can determine, and so was not a great deal that he could teach us in that respect, but we were learning basic English.

> *And was it a proper classroom then?*

> Well yes, in every sense of the word, it was a classroom. We had desks and, well not school desk type, they were tables and chairs and so on, and the maybe two or three to a table and that's how we were. We learned to speak a little bit, sing a little bit and it was quite enjoyable, I enjoyed it; I think it lasted six months."[6]

Another Hungarian John Nugi who's journey to Forest Town was via Brigg and Chesterfield also recalled these lessons were in the Hostel.

> "...we have a school lesson with proper teachers on the site. In the morning we learn, sometimes afternoon you know; we learn the language...Oh yes, it was a proper classroom; tables, blackboard, you name it. We have [to] write, teacher write it down, we have to read it, we have to spell it to get on with it. Oh yes, we have books...English and Hungarian books...It was a female teacher living somewhere Ladybrook way, I'm not sure exactly, but she and the gentleman teacher...I can't remember his name, ...we have to learn hard to get on with..."[7]

Hungarian refugees with their lady Teacher

Not everyone found the classroom situation ideal as Brenda Sandor recalled. Michael, her Hungarian husband always felt he learnt more English from listening to people than he did from the teacher at the Hostel. When Brenda first met Michael the language was a bit of a problem, they used to try and converse in English. On one occasion when they met some of his friends, they began all talking in Hungarian, which was easier for them than English, but not for Brenda who threatened to leave if they were going to talk in Hungarian. After this he used to try and converse so that she could be part of it. This situation must have been common with many couples of mixed race, and work colleagues at that time.

There are obviously adjustments to be made when people move to a new country and for the Hungarians one was getting used to the food and drink, especially drinking tea.

> "When we came first oh we couldn't drink it. We say interpreter, coffee please. So of course our interpreter try to explain to us that this is India tea. We drinking tea back home, but we don't use milk…just tea and a bit of sugar or lemon."[8]

> "Took some getting used to tea because being a coffee drinker…tea that I could remember was nothing like the tea we got there…you see I never, I could never remember drinking tea with milk."[9]

In the first hostel Charles Dery stayed in they had Hungarian food cooked. However -

> "…Forest Town it was a different thing, because it was a mixed community you see, it was English food, English stews and I think usually Yorkshire puddings and roasts and things like that, so just normal food…I can remember going in, and oh it's not stew again. …But it was good clean food…I could eat it seven days a week, so it didn't matter to me, it was food, it filled the need.

> We used to be charged for it, yes. Initially I think we had a sum of money given to us every week during our schooling period, but I'm not certain of the amount. And out of that used to be deducted so much for food and accommodation, and the rest was yours, which amounted to about three pounds or something like that in them days, maybe a bit less, but I can't remember the exact amount."[10]

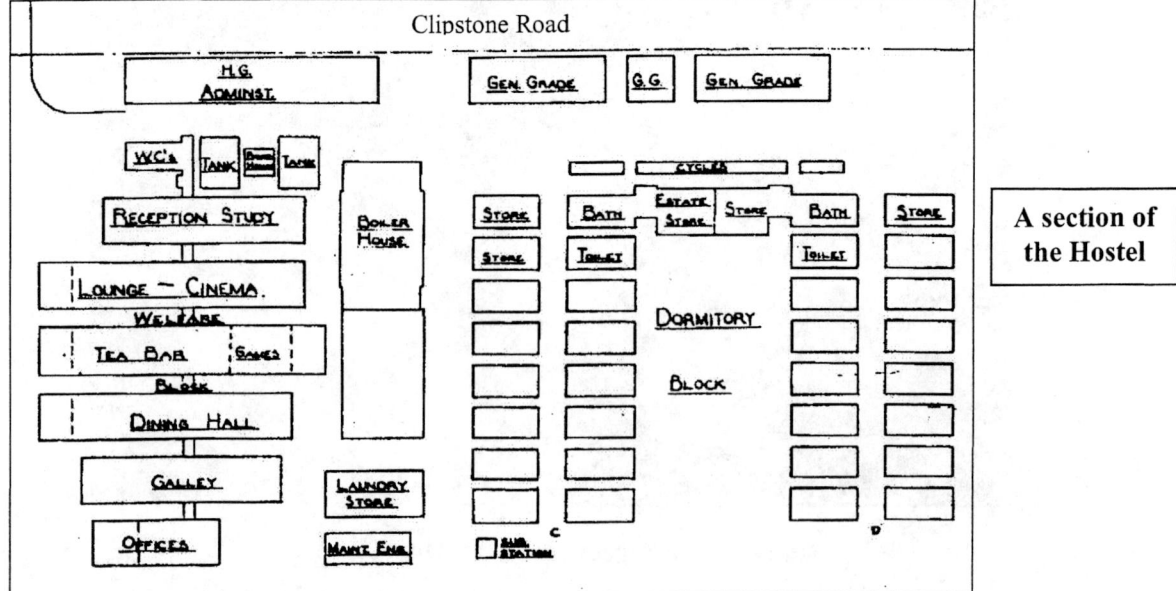

A section of the Hostel

First impressions remain with people and like many other occupants had done before them, the Hungarian refugees also considered the Forest Town Hostel was a good place to live:

> "…excellent, we had good food…it was only basic with today's standards, but it was clean and we had a shower and bathing facilities. There was a nice dining room where you could go and there was also a community room where you could go and play cards or chess or whatever took your fancy, and so it wasn't too bad. It was quite good. …
>
> …we did share one dormitory. Joe our other friend he was in another one further down the corridor. There was a long corridor, on either side of the corridor there were the living quarters.…And each, I think there were about sixteen or there maybe less, I'm not certain how many persons it accommodated…just a bed and a little locker and that was it, it was very very basic. It was nice and comfortable and it was a lot better than sleeping in the refugee hostel elsewhere…they were clean and nice, but they were very basic and nothing to write home about."[11]
>
> "Well, I'll be honest with you, it was comfortable…there was plenty of hot water, it was clean, every week they changed the sheets. The cleaner was in the room you know you didn't have to do nothing, clean or anything. Every week they clean sheets, plenty of hot water, food was perfect for £3.50.
>
> *So were you in long dormitories or where did you sleep?*
>
> Well…the room was a long room, I think it was ten of us, I'm not sure exactly, eight or ten of us, which it wasn't over crowded. We all have a comfortable wardrobe and a bed, and we had a bathroom, everything…it was a really comfortable."[12]

Both residents and staff remember basic medical facilities. There was a room where people could be given treatment for minor ailments and the Doctor visiting if he was needed. A kindness by one of the receptionist was on one occasion misinterpreted;

> "After the Hungarian revolution of course we had all the Hungarians frightened to death, and I asked one of them who had got a headache if he wanted a tablet and he wouldn't take it, he thought I was trying to poison him."[13]

When the Hungarians first arrived they had to be registered into the Hostel. Lily Wright (now Kurnatowski)[14] who had worked there in the late 1940s returned to work in the offices.

> "Yes, we actually booked them in you know, we had to sit with the police on a row of 'em, I can't remember what their names were now. We had a lot to do with them two in particular, I think they were detectives actually…we all sat at this table and we was issuing them like with the identity things and all that."

Lily (Wright) Kurnatowski

For the Hungarians this registration system was not strange.

"You see where I come from we had a permanent one, it was a way of life for us. A book of registration book, in which you had to have your every detail of your life, whether you were a single person, where you worked, what was your occupation, have you been in the Army, have you been in custody, you know, have you had any form. So it was just like being at home, to be perfectly honest with you…I had no qualms about it whatsoever, the only thing that used to bug me, was having to go to the police station to report."[15] [This had to be done on a regular basis for a number of years]

Marjorie Smith

The confidence of the staff was soon gained however as Marjorie Smith recalled:

"One incident I can remember…was with a Hungarian boy. When they were going to go down the pits and our miners wouldn't accept them they still had to be paid £8 a week. So one came to me and said, "What's this on my ticket?" I said "That's Income Tax." He said, "Well I don't want to join that club." I said, "No I don't but I'm still in it!"

Unfortunately for some of the men intending to be miners there was a problem of acceptance and work.

"…the local unions, Mining Union decided that they weren't going to let the refugees down after all because of some dispute or other with the Government about employing foreign labour when there is plenty of the local population that can be employed down the mines. So they refused to allow them down the pit…only the Nottinghamshire Mining Union, elsewhere they weren't so bad, they weren't so strict. Some [refugees] decided that they not going to stay, [in Nottinghamshire], whatever happen they'll go down the mine. They travelled elsewhere, down Wales and up Scotland and Yorkshire where the unions weren't so strict about letting them work down the coal mines."[16]

"…because what happened here you see the NUM because of government, NUM refused to let us go down so we was pressing to the interpreter. Another Hungarian named John, I forget his other name [said] we can't go on like this we got no pocket money, so of course the pressing of government and NUM negotiating hard, have to do something because we was uproaring, …of course they realise they have to do something. Some of us don't got a decent clothes. Of course the Red Cross did the best they possibly can, and when we first crossed the border of Austria the government bought us new shoes, new clothes, new coat, new shirt, everything, but when you talking about 250,000 of course the government said I can't do it. So you had to turn to the rest for support. The Red Cross did their best, but still as a young lad you need fag, you want to go for a drink etc, …we not satisfied. They put it to the governor in that Hostel, whatever you call it, and they pressed on pit saying if you not going to do something there is going to be uproar…so they say right. I think there was £9 a week as pocket money and we have to pay out of that £3.50 or £3 to keep us."[17]

While this situation was obviously not easy for the Hungarians, it was also difficult for some of the local miners to accept.

"Well I remember 1956 when they had a trouble in Hungary, a lot of the Hungarian refugees apparently come to England, and there was so many in Forest Town Hostel. …It was a bit of problem with them, because we were working and we get about six or seven pound a week wages for working; they get same amount of money as us from Social Security, and the lads they didn't like that, you see. But after a couple of months it dispersed, they either went on other job or another part of country or something like that."[18]

Despite the NCB and the NUM agreeing to recruit Hungarians for the mines, this was not successful for 'as in the earlier schemes many local branches of the NUM exercised their right to refuse to work with foreign recruits.'[19] By the end of 1957 out of 4,186 Hungarians recruited and trained by the NCB only 731 had been placed in employment and not all of them were at collieries.[20] Working at a colliery did not mean the men would be doing the job they had anticipated.

"I myself decided because I couldn't work down, what do you call it the mine here, I'll get what employment there was. …An acquaintance, an English gentleman who lived in Forest Town on George Street, Charlie Pickard by the name, we used to go to Prince Charles almost every weekend, just for a chat and a drink of beer…and see different faces. …This gentleman used to be there because it was his local, and consequently we got in conversation with him…well I mentioned that you know we'd like to go and work somewhere…he was a canteen manager at Clipstone Briquette Works.

I've never heard of such things myself before, so well why not, I'll give it a go, so anyway he took me in that particular Monday and straight away I was set on. So by the following day I was working there, only as a labourer, shovelling and whatever job was available, or needed to be done, emptying wagons of coal dust or slurry, coal dust the machines were using, they mixing it with coal tar, coal pitch as it was called. I was working, I was happy as a mud lark."[21]

Some men were employed at local collieries but not as an underground miner.

"…after that I realised I was never going to be a miner and I first took a labour job. I then learned the language by practising, and then I got an engineering job."

So you weren't a miner at all?

"…I worked for the mining seven years, something like that…I was working Welbeck pit and Clipstone pit, but in 1960 when I went to Clipstone pit, I was…not direct underground worker, …used to be called a powder shop [possibly power loader] repairing pit machines…"[22]

Other men such as Michael turned to another trade.

> "...yes, as a painter and decorator yes he used to go round 'em all, they had like on contracts...and they go to all the different hospitals he went to everyone I think and then he painted Clipstone Headstocks. He used to come down - like, they call it abseiling, and he used to frighten secretaries to death, cause they used to think he'd thrown himself off the top...he got told off and had to come down."[23]

Clipstone Headstocks 1997

While the Hungarians were living at the Forest Town Hostel they also used the local shops, and like many other people, discovered the corner shop, near to Sherwood Hall Garage. Additionally a grocer's shop near to the Prince Charles Public House is remembered for its supply of continental food. The newsagents was where the men could buy their cigarettes, purchasing newspapers that were all in English did not appeal to the men who were struggling to learn the language. For those that enjoyed an ice cream the owners of the newsagent shop set up a stall at the weekends where ice cream wafers were sold.

A happy group of Hungarians

For those who wanted it they could find recreation either at the Hostel or in the local community. For liquid refreshment the Hungarians had the choice of local Pubs, The Ravensdale, and the Prince Charles or they would walk into Mansfield. In the Hostel there was a community room where card, chess or other games could be played. One or two enjoyable dances are remembered, and sometimes the men had their own musical entertainment, talented drum and harmonica players were recalled.

Early in 1957 when the facilities at the Forest Town Hostel (along with those at Alfreton) were reviewed, and extensions authorised, it had been anticipated that hundreds of Hungarians would move into the area. A total 1,206 additional places were made available. However within a few months it was evident that the predicted number of refugees had not materialised. On the '6th July only 433 Hungarians (195 at Forest Town and 238 at Alfreton) were in residence.'[24] The indications were that this would continue to decline. Not only had there been fewer Hungarian men come to the Hostel than envisaged, some of the occupants had only stayed a short time. They had moved out after finding independent lodgings.

The figures quoted are just for the Hungarians and although the Hostel still had residents of other nationalities staying there, the indications are that the overall number of residents was decreasing. The general housing situation was improving and many of the people who had benefitted from the hostel-type accommodation, were now able to move out and purchase their own house or obtain rented properties.

As people moved out it caused a few problems at the General Post Office, they had previously been able to put all the letters for the Hostel in one bag and not worry about the many foreign surnames. The head postmaster Jack Wakefield recalled that:

> "…Redirecting the correspondence…they'd got such strange names that we often got into little tangles with them."

This was however not a major problem and the post office soon got adjusted to delivering more letters in the community and less to the Hostel.

When the anticipated number of Hungarian refugees did not materialise at the Forest Town Hostel from 1957 onwards, it was possibly the beginning of the decline. It was just two years later in 1959, when the National Coal Board made the ultimate decision to close the Hostel, and in doing so ended a fifteen-year era of fascinating history.

Notes

[1]	PRO COAL 75/2460
[2]	Chad 6 December 1956
[3]	PRO COAL 23/369
[4]	PRO COAL 75/2460
[5]	Chad 13 December 1956
[6]	Charles Lewis Dery
[7]	Jainos (John) Nugi
[8]	Jainos (John) Nugi
[9]	Charles Lewis Dery
[10]	Charles Lewis Dery
[11]	Charles Lewis Dery
[12]	Jainos (John) Nugi
[13]	Marjorie Smith
[14]	Lily Wright married Maximillian Kurnatowski they later changed their name to Kent
[15]	Charles Lewis Dery
[16]	Charles Lewis Dery
[17]	Jainos (John) Nugi
[18]	Eugan Megdalewitsch
[19]	W Ashworth *The History of the British Coal Industry Vol 5 pg 164*
[20]	W Ashworth *The History of the British Coal Industry Vol 5 pg 164*
[21]	Charles Lewis Dery
[22]	Jainos (John) Nugi
[23]	Brenda Sandor
[24]	PRO COAL 23/369

CLOSURE & THE FINAL CHAPTER

When it was announced that the Forest Town Miners' Hostel would close on the 10th October 1959, it really was the end of a most intriguing and unusual era in one village's local history. The background to the whole story was war and coal. War, that disrupted the lives of many people. People from all different backgrounds that needed accommodation for whatever reason, and coal, that was such an essential ingredient of industry, and yet was dependent on manpower to produce it.

In the beginning the Hostel was built because homes were needed for miners, and ironically at the end, once again homes were being sought for miners. When officials at the National Coal Board, East Midland Division Headquarters, spoke to local newspapers about the closure they said that an effort was being made to find homes for the remaining 200 residents, still at the Hostel. Requests were to be sent to miners in No 2 Area NCB asking if they could offer accommodation.[1]

The Hostel closed in October and within two months it had been handed back to the Ministry of Works.[2] The events over the following years are still relatively unknown, the time constraints of the Millennium Award Project have not allowed for the in-depth research needed to discover this.

However, there are various memories of mostly unrecorded oral history. Adults remember that when they were children they played on the empty site sometimes building a den or tunnel. The collapse of one such tunnel was recalled, fortunately no one was hurt.

People recall a sale of equipment at which many a bargain was purchased - a cast iron bath which is still in use today. Royal Doulton sinks bought for ten bob [50p]. One lady had a deep white sink, bricks to put the sink on, and a wooden draining board to make a gate with.

Huts, window frames, and bricks found new homes on the village allotments. Additionally bricks were used to make bases for pigeon lofts or walls in people's gardens.

Allotments in Forest Town – November 1991

One former Hostel resident that had moved into his own home recalled:

> "…We had to do lot of work repairing…I hear that they're pulling Hostel down. So I went to go and have a look at what going off on there…it was a dump, and they were selling what they could. They were selling wood and whatever was around the camp, and I got some doors from there, they just fit this property. …I took a barrow that time [to collect them in].[3]

The people who still have some of these items will not consider them as history, and yet as such they are. Additionally there are people for whom Forest Town or the Hostel has played a double part in their lives. People who themselves, (or their spouse), once resided at the Hostel, in later years moved to live in houses or bungalows that were built on the Hostel site. Many years after a former Derbyshire Police Force recruit had passed out from the No 3 Training Centre in 1946, he returned with his wife to live in Forest Town.[4]

Forest Town was the home of the first Police Training Centre after the Second World War, despite it being designated No 3. Another policeman who was at the Forest Town Centre rose through the ranks:

> "…He had just returned from the RAF. Sergeant Knights later became the Chief Constable of the West Midland's Force; shortly afterwards he became Sir Philip Knight[s] and he's now Lord Knight[s]."[5]

For the people who were Bevin Boys at Forest Town and elsewhere, recognition of their war service may have come late, and some will not be aware there is now a well-established Bevin Boys Association. On discovering this, Bert Allott was quick to join and become a proud member. This was an added bonus to our Millennium Award Project.

Additionally, interviewing a gentleman whose memory and speech had been affected through a stroke was for us very rewarding, and a tremendous achievement for him.

While we did not discover anyone who was evacuated with the epileptic children we did make contact with the school in Lingfield, Surrey where the epileptic children were evacuated from, and learnt it is now The National Centre For Young People With Epilepsy. A book written for their centenary in 1997, 'One Hundred Years of St Piers' by Susan Turner a member of staff there, does refer to the children coming to Forest Town.

Since the start of this project last autumn we have been in contact with, and met some wonderful people. We have additionally become very aware that behind each of them is another individual story. The families of some of the people interviewed have suddenly become aware of areas of their parents' life, and their 'family history' has taken on a new dimension. The interest and enthusiasm of the people who have taken part has been very encouraging. Their contribution means the fifteen years of the Forest Town Miners' Hostel's existence is not lost in time. It is now recorded for future generations to learn about.

Many hours of tape recording have taken place, and numerous photographs have been loaned for copying, each memory or photo is part of the wider historical picture. While it has not been possible to use everything in the finished book or video associated with this project, they are all being preserved in the Nottingham Living History Archive at Nottingham Library.

The Hostel site as it looked in the spring of 2002

Where the Hostel once stood is a large housing estate, a Police Station that opened in 1965 and whose future is today unknown,[6] and also a Library officially opened in 1964. It is where the project started with the children of Forest Town Primary School investigating the buildings, and where the voyage of discovery started. It is fitting that the Library will now have an addition to its local history information, which will be there for others to read and maybe in time even add to, for no local history is ever complete.

The final word will be left to the children of Forest Town Primary School, who on the 22nd May 2002 after listening to our discoveries about the Hostel and its occupants said,
"Fascinating!"

Notes

1   Mansfield Chronicle 10 Sep 1959
2   PRO COAL 23/369
3   Eugen Megdalewitsch
4   Frank Smith sadly now deceased.
5   Frank Hanford [also recalled by other people]
6   The Police Station closed earlier this year.

BIBLIOGRAPHY

Ashworth W   The History of the British Coal Industry
                         Vol 5   (Oxford 1986)

Beal G./Grisewood J   *Factbook of the 20th Century*   (1995)

Cook J &
T Rowland-Entwistle   *Factbook of British History*   (Leicester Press 1984)

Englert J L   *General Anders*   (1990)

Griffin A   Mining in the East Midlands   (1971)

Taylor
 Lord of Mansfield   *Uphill All The Way*   (1972)

Taylor W   *The Forgotten Conscript*   (Durham 1988)

Turner S   *One Hundred Years of St Piers*   (Lingfield 1997)

Withers B   *Nottinghamshire Constabulary*   (Huddersfield 1989)

Readers Digest   *Life On The Home Front*   (1983)

                      Eden Camp, The Peoples War 1939-45 (Eden Camp 1992)

Occasional Paper

Carey G   *On Becoming a Bevin Boy in Nottinghamshire 1944* (1999)

Newspapers

Mansfield & Kirkby Chronicle
Mansfield Chronicle Advertiser
Mansfield & North Notts Advertiser